"This book is invaluable
pates in teams. Whether yo
this book leads you through a process that will make both you and your
team more focused, more productive, and more cohesive. It will give
you renewed excitement about what your team can and will accomplish
if you follow his step by step process."

— Scott Foster, business owner

"Finally, someone has put into print the secrets for today's successful
business leader. Obviously, the old autocratic management style does
not work in today's world. I have learned by working with Michael
Miller that the more we empower our teams, the more responsibility
they will take on. In today's "right sized" organization, we must energize our teams to perform to the max. The weekly team meeting ("People Connection") does an incredible job of energizing the entire team.
It improves morale, service, quality, and productivity. As a manager,
I don't know how to fix all of the daily problems, but I can create the
right environment for my team to succeed. Connecting with the team
is my first priority; understanding who they are, what excites them,
how to engage them, and giving them the proper tools. They no longer
look for me to solve all the problems....we share a common goal...they
know what needs to get done. I am moved by this quote: "Leaders
don't force people to follow them...they invite them on a journey." I
highly recommend "The Infinite Power of Teams" by Michael Miller."

— Dennis Wells, VP

"A beacon for ANY team endeavor. Read it. Share it. It works!!!
More than a self help for the business sector, this book could revolu-
tionize public education for example. It really is for any & all teams."

— Tracy Newsom, Production Supervisor

"*The Infinite Power Of Teams* isn't written by a college professor offering
theory and no practical experience. Mike Miller has been on the firing
line for years with a variety of workplace teams. He has developed a
time-tested process that works if you're willing to apply the three steps
necessary for a more caring, cohesive, collaborative and committed
team. Read this book slowly. Study it carefully. And, most importantly,
implement an action plan immediately to get the results you want from
your team."

— Dick Biggs, Professional Speaker & Author
Of Burn Brightly Without Burning Out

ISBN: 1-4196-9272-0

ISBN-13: 9781419692727

Library of Congress Control Number: 2008902170

Michael Miller

THE INFINITE POWER OF TEAMS

How Organizations and Individuals Achieve Greatness Together

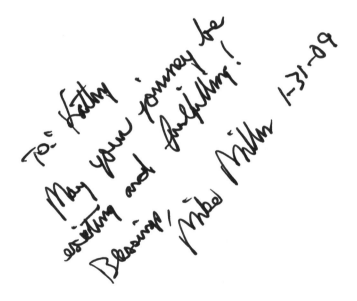

To: Kathy
May your journey be exciting and fulfilling!
Blessings! Mike Miller 1-31-09

ACKNOWLEDGEMENTS

I want to especially thank my wife, Lynn, for her patience, love, and support through all the many trying years and hundreds of hours of discussions that incubated this book. I am also deeply indebted to Roy and Marjorie Miller, who by being such wonderful parents, prepared me to absorb and master these powerful principles. My editor and coach, Joy Barrett, was indispensable as a teacher, mentor, and cheerleader.

I had a long list of editors, reviewers, and discussion partners who spent countless hours reading, writing comments, and challenging me. Even the ones who didn't read the manuscript caused me to redouble my efforts to produce a book that would grab and hold a reader's attention. The following people are standouts I want to thank:

Leslie Bindloss – a talented author who helped and encouraged me.

Steve Craver – a wonderful and treasured mentor and encourager.

Scott Foster – his help was invaluable in learning how to write this book.

Clay Fulghum – a great editor who led me to a breakthrough in clarification.

Marshall Jones – so few edits, but so much impact.

Mark King – a very perceptive, steady and reliable encourager.

Traci Martin – a vibrant intellect who cast a new light on the book.

Tracy Newsom – a gifted communicator whose honesty contributed so much.

Greg Poupard – a mentor and a sage who tells it just like it is in a caring way.

Bucky Rosenbaum – helped me to accomplish the focus I was striving for.

Bob Zwart – a wonderful friend with an abundance of energy and insight.

Mike Miller

TABLE OF CONTENTS
The Infinite Power of Teams
How Organizations and Individuals Achieve Greatness Together

An Overview of the Process

Learning and Practicing the Process

Understanding and Mastering the Process

INTRODUCTION

Infinite power is available to all teams and it takes us where we never dreamed possible. Team members, leaders, business owners, stockholders, and customers from all walks of life need a different and energizing approach to working together. There is a Process that will take – no, it will shake the center stage of your team. Center stage will shake when you hear the stories of teams that have blown through the limits. Center stage will shake when you learn how to apply the simple principles of this exciting and powerful Process to your own teams.

I've been involved with a large number of improvement programs and processes, and this one is different from all the rest. It's different because it captures the heart and soul of a team, and this heart is what drives the team to ever increasing levels of performance. It's also different because it focuses on mindset and a one-hour weekly meeting that replaces a number of others, rather than on a collection of tools and skills.

I was fortunate to have been involved directly in the beginnings of this Process more than 20 years ago. Our team can claim no credit for inventing it, however, because creating something was not our intent. We had a work assignment and keeping that assignment simple and unchanged was just the way our minds worked, not brilliant foresight. Simplicity and consistency turned out to be the keys to our success. And surprisingly, the simpler the Process evolved over the years, the more thrilling the team performances became. Evolution from simple to simpler is not the course most processes take. That's one thing that makes this Process so unusual.

This Process will astound you. "Unbelievable" and "I'm blown away" are the "technical" terms most observers use when describing the performance of teams using it. Every time I think I have seen the best-ever performance, the next team tops it – ten different teams, ten different times! The teams ranged from 20 to 500 in size, from service to manufacturing, and even a church congregation. I was in a key leadership position in each one of these teams, and an employee in all but two. A mindset change and a one-hour weekly meeting describes the Process that enabled these teams to excel – it wasn't extra work.

I believe the power of this Process comes from being in much greater harmony with how we're designed as human beings. The principles that make this Process work were discovered and developed by far greater minds than mine. Ancient philosophers and leaders began this journey of discovery and development that was continued by such recent luminaries as Dr. W. Edward Deming, Stephen Covey, Tom Paterson, John Maxwell, Jim Collins, Ken Blanchard, and Peter Drucker. Though the principles have been widely shared, this Process is unique as far as I know. It's a reformulation of these time-honored principles into a Process that can be used by today's highly chaotic and stressed world that desperately needs a solution that works.

This Process works in _**any organization**_ that has people and processes. Any time people must work together to accomplish a common goal, they must follow some kind of process. Every organization must divide up the work and establish communication channels – unfortunately, this doesn't always work well. Communication channels and division of work are examples of processes. Whether it's driving a ball to the goal, serving the customer, educating the student, or building a product, they all involve people and processes.

You'll hear stories about a church and an insurance agency, even though most of the stories are about manufacturing. If this Process can work in manufacturing, it can work anywhere. People are people, no matter what their occupation.

I use real-life stories to show you this Process isn't just some pretty talk, fancy theory, or soothing philosophy that is a useless luxury in this world of problems, pressures, disappointments, frustrations, and cynicism. This Process works in spite of all this negative stuff *and* without ever having to solve all the nagging problems we want to rid ourselves of. Yes, you read that right! Focusing on the goal allows us to escape the work and drudgery of solving problems. Amazingly, most of today's problems seem to simply disappear when an exciting goal or vision replaces problems as a team's focus. Many become irrelevant, and the important ones turn into opportunities to reach the goal – an important attitude change for a team.

I fully expect that my experiences will pale in comparison with what many of you will be able to accomplish with your teams – because this Process builds on success. The vision of this book is to unleash the infinite power of teams for every team member, customer, leader, coach, owner, stockholder, and board member in this country. The steps are yawningly simple: *think it, believe it, work it, and then experience it. The journey, on the other hand, is an adventure that you will never forget!* It starts on page one. I will be with you to the last page and would love to hear what you do with it.

Just one note before you turn the page: The names of all facilities and individuals used in each of these stories (all true) have been changed out of respect for the individuals and companies involved.

AN OVERVIEW OF THE PROCESS

This is the first of three sections in this book. Each section builds on the one before it. The readers who simply want to familiarize themselves with the Process and how it works can do that by completing the first section. The readers who want to be a contributing team member should complete the first two sections. The readers who want to give it 100 percent, as either a team member or team leader, should complete all three sections. You will impress yourself...and your team, if you read and apply it all.

Each section covers the entire process at a progressively higher level. I assure you that no one will get short of breath as we climb. In fact, the breathing becomes easier because the air gets fresher the higher we go. For those who complete all three sections, the wrap-up at the end should be a mountain-top experience. Mastery, as you will soon see, is surprisingly intuitive and user-friendly, so let's dive in! You and your team deserve it.

⌒ CHAPTER 1: THE TEAM

He who cannot change the very fabric of his thought will never be able
to change reality, and will never, therefore, make any progress.

– Anwar Sadat

Teamwork is the only thing that can save us. When faced with the most extreme tests of survival imaginable, we need the ultimate defense. But is teamwork alone sufficient? Could we possibly succeed with no other tool? Let's start by considering a study related by Peter Miller in the July 2007 issue of the National Geographic:[1]

Karsten Heuer, a wildlife biologist, and his wife, Leanne Allison, followed the vast Porcupine caribou herd for five months in 2003. They followed the herd for more than a thousand miles, documenting the migration from their winter range in Canada's northern Yukon Territory to calving grounds in Alaska's Arctic National Wildlife Refuge.

They were so awed by this experience that they found it difficult to describe in words how this herd traveled together. They moved like a "cloud shadow" over the landscape as if each animal was perfectly coordinated with the others.

One day, Heuer and Allison noticed a wolf sneaking up on the caribou. "As soon as the wolf got within a certain distance of the caribou, the herd's alertness just skyrocketed," Heuer says. The herd froze until the wolf moved a hundred yards closer. Suddenly, Heuer went on, "The nearest caribou turned and ran, and that response moved like a wave through the entire herd until they were all running. Animals closest to the wolf at the back end of the herd looked like a blanket unraveling and tattering, which, from the wolf's perspective, must have been extremely confusing."

Author Peter Miller went on to say, "the wolf chased one caribou after another, losing ground with each change of target. In the end, the herd escaped over the ridge, and the wolf was left panting and gulping snow. *For each caribou, the stakes couldn't have been higher, yet the herd's evasive maneuvers displayed not panic, but precision.* [Italics mine.] (Imagine the chaos if a hungry wolf were released into a crowd of people). Every caribou knew when it was time to run and in which direction to go, even if it didn't know exactly why ...each animal was following simple rules..."

Teamwork alone saved the caribou. *Teamwork alone will save our teams also.* Add tools and technology to the mix and our potential is infinite.

Why use caribou as an example of teamwork? There's a lot we can learn, and have learned from nature. We'll soon see how our human experiences are beginning to converge with nature's lessons on teamwork. Note the observation about how the caribou were following simple rules. Human teamwork can benefit greatly from simplicity, also.

Wolves are pressing at America's doors today. American business performance is not faring well against global competition, and other countries are getting our jobs at an alarming rate. Compelling arguments say this is healthy in the long run, but, arguments – just as compelling – say many jobs should have never left our borders. Pessimism is rampant about America's ability to stay in the lead. America's future is uncertain.

Job dissatisfaction is as high as it's ever been. A shocking 75 percent of employees would change jobs today if they could. This statistic is supported by numerous studies from a number of sources ranging from a staffing company to major newspapers[2]. Many of these studies argue that the workforce has changed significantly since 9/11/2001. The abundant observations of low morale, disengaged employees, low productivity, and circulating resumes readily validates this 75 percent. Unfortunately, even if everyone who wanted a new job got it, we would still have a high level of job dissatisfaction because the main causal factor would still be with us. The cause: *Most organizations simply have not won the loyalty and commitment of their employees.*

Organization management wants this loyalty and commitment badly, but is not doing the right things to get it. They think they can get it from high profile improvement programs that involve the employees, from charismatic leaders who inspire a following, and from strategic decision-making that builds confidence. Even though each of these can produce impressive results, none are self-sustaining or long-lasting. *Winning the heart and soul of a team is the only way to significant and lasting success.*

Most managers believe how important this is, but they also believe that they can win this commitment in spite of the probable outcome of their practices. They are like gamblers who know the odds favor the casino, but they play anyway. Many take it to an extreme and say simply that better employees with better attitudes is all they need. Given that 80 percent of the labor pool is already unhappy, their chance of getting those ideal employees is very low.

The opportunity is huge. I have seen ten organizations in unbroken succession go through dramatic transformations simply by winning the heart and soul of the team. The Process we followed has produced gains of at least 20 to 30 percent in just about every measure within three to twelve months. Everyone notices, and everyone becomes excited about these transformations – the customers, the stockholders, the employees, and even visitors.

Since most teams are not able to take advantage of this opportunity, everyone gets into the blame game when things don't go right. The bosses blame the employees and the employees blame the boss. It is a well-known fact that most employees leave their job because of the boss. We could go with the flow, just blame the bosses, and save the rest of this book for something else. But wait. Could there be another reason for all of this unhappiness?

Could it be the bosses are products of team dysfunctions rather than the cause of them? Could it be they are only doing what the system has trained and rewarded them for? Could it be that bosses want the same things that

team members do? The answer is yes to all three questions. Starting with
wants, team members and bosses share the following:

∞   To hold the gains on improvement projects and programs.

∞   To improve morale and make the workplace exciting.

∞   To improve quality.

∞   To improve productivity.

∞   To improve employee engagement.

∞   To excite the customer.

∞   To excite the stockholders.

∞   To be the best.

There is a major misconnection, or misunderstanding, between bosses and team members. Let's turn to the bosses and see what we can do
about it.

Bosses and managers become leaders when they adopt a bigger picture
than their job description. They become leaders when they stop simply
chopping trees in the woods they're in, and start looking around to see if
there are better woods to chop in. They become leaders when they truly
start *supporting* their teams, instead of just their performance objectives.
If a team is falling short, then the leader takes responsibility for the short-
fall and the path to success. The path to success starts with bridging the
misconnect between the leader and the team.

CONNECTING THE LEADERS AND TEAM MEMBERS

Connecting team leaders and team members is easier than most of
us think. This can be accomplished with a simple Process that pulls a
team together in a powerful way. *We can actually work in a way
that will genuinely excite the employees, the stockholders, and the
customers <u>simultaneously.</u>*

This Process is called the *"People Connection"*, and it's a one-hour,
weekly all-staff meeting that does an incredible job of energizing the people

on your team or organization. Don't call me crazy for calling another meeting yet, because this meeting actually eliminates the need for many other meetings. *The People Connection is far simpler and more practical than any other improvement process because it <u>relies almost entirely on mindset and a simple three topic meeting</u>, not a complex set of tools and activities.* Our work life is too complicated already. What we need is something to simplify it.

THE PEOPLE CONNECTION

1. *Leaders think differently about their teams (different mindset).*
   a. One team, not a collection of individuals.
   b. Lead the 60 percent in the middle (of the performance ranking).
   c. Fill the team members' need to be great and to be a part of something great.

2. *One-hour meeting once per week with all team members. Standing agenda:*
   a. Discuss the vision. (5 minutes)
   b. Discuss how to achieve the vision and how the team members will implement the steps to reach it. (50 minutes)
   c. Answer the questions what are we doing well and what can we do better? (5 minutes)

The People Connection will work for *any* organization or team that has people and processes. *We typically think this applies only to business, especially manufacturing, but this Process works just as well in churches, insurance agencies, and in many other organizations.* I believe it will work with sports teams, non-profits, volunteer groups, hospitals, schools and colleges as well. Anytime people work together using even the simplest of processes, there's a better way to get results. The People Connection creates exactly the right environment for that to happen.

This book is intended for every manager, boss, leader and team member. It's not easy to find a fit for everybody, because people and teams have such a variety of dysfunctions. You will no doubt recognize many of these dysfunctions in "Dilbert", the popular comic strip by Scott Adams which so accurately portrays the workplace.

One episode of Dilbert shows the boss being transferred to a new job where he is responsible for improving morale. As soon as his old group finds out they no longer report to him, morale skyrockets and the CEO thinks the boss is a genius. Another episode shows Alice abusing another team member in a meeting, calling him "fly bait" and threatening to pound his "head so hard you'll have to remove your pants to read". She then asks if she's missed anything about teamwork, having arrived late to the meeting. At the same moment and in the chair next to her, Dilbert is asking Scott Adams, the author of the comic strip, where he gets his material.[3]

One typical dysfunction that stands out is how much people seem to do or say without thinking. Do you think the guy who cut you off in traffic today did it intentionally? More than likely he was totally oblivious, even though we usually write it off as rudeness. We claim we never do things like this, but how would we know for sure? Lapses in attention and awareness are, by definition, something we're oblivious of.

Why am I going here? That's a good question. The good answer is that removing blind spots, or that oblivion we all have, is an important part of the People Connection. A team who flies blind, even if only a little bit, will not live up to its potential.

This oblivion can show up as patterns of behavior or decisions that create problems with people we work with. We usually have teammates and bosses who point those problems out to us; and these are commonly called criticisms. I have met very few people who are keen on receiving criticisms, however.

The bad news is that no one has come up with a better system. So maybe we just need to accept that it works, and look at the improvements that result from criticisms as "gifts". Aren't the pain and humiliation usually worth the courage it takes to positively react to criticisms? A twisted mind would want to get as many of these "gifts" as possible, and a twisted mind has advantages as we will soon see. Wouldn't the person who **benefited** most from these gifts be admired? Though this system is bittersweet, it works great in eliminating blind spots.

Everyone doesn't benefit equally from this system, unfortunately. Bosses are frequently left out of these gift exchanges. Today's culture has placed managers, supervisors, and leaders <u>over</u> the team members getting the job done. This in effect stifles the flow of gifts from team members to bosses and team leaders. It stifles them because someone of "higher status" deserves respect, and respect gets twisted into meaning subordinates can't make the leader feel vulnerable or uncomfortable by communicating criticisms, even if they're constructive.

Even worse, team members go overboard in showing "respect" by feeding the boss's ego by telling him or her what they want to hear. Respect also gets distorted into meaning that the boss must be right because they're the boss. "How can a peon like me question the boss's thinking?" The disconnected boss is now out on a limb and has no way of knowing if it will snap off one day and plunge them to an uncertain fate.

Okay, now everything's fair since the bosses have been shorted gifts from the team, and the team has been shorted good leadership. What "genius" designed this system anyway?

Believe it or not, this system of bosses and subordinates is a pretty good one. It works great for the military. The "boss", or general, has to make quick and effective decisions, and usually has most of the information necessary to do that well. It wouldn't make sense to hold a team meeting to decide how to defend a hill after the enemy suddenly attacks. When the U.S. Industrial Revolution began to hit stride early in the 20th century, most organizations successfully used the proven and successful military model.

However, the old military model does not work well in this modern age of complexity, tough information challenges, overflowing email and voicemail boxes, and much higher standards and expectations. It's crucial that the leader and the team work together as one, and this can only happen through ***strong connections*** between the two. The leader needs to see what the team sees, and the team needs to see what the leader sees – as precisely as humanly possible. A tool for measuring this connectivity appears on page 9. The leader and each team member should fill out this assessment anonymously. The team leaders will be able to see from this assessment how much the system has hurt their connection with their team.

The misconnection is pretty predictable. Today, most teams with a good boss will rate themselves about a five or six and the boss's score will be pretty close. If the boss has had training or study in the more progressive leadership tools, then the boss will probably rate their teams an eight or nine. However, the teams working for bosses like this will more than likely still rate themselves a five or six because of connectivity problems. Connectivity depends on much more than just conventional training, so the boss who *thinks* he or she is leading better isn't necessarily getting the best results. It's the difference – or misconnection – between what the team sees and the boss sees that concerns us most. Fix this gap and the team will find its way to higher performance.

This assessment takes just a couple of minutes to complete, so this would be a good time to do that. Readers are encouraged to take this assessment by themselves, if they are not taking it with their team. This tool is designed for virtually everyone on a team of any kind. ***Managers, supervisors, and team leaders need to consider themselves a team member, not as a boss when filling out this assessment.*** Don't put names on your paper, since they won't be graded and handed back. Instead of handing them back, the team leader will study them to see how the team sees itself, versus how the leader sees it. The assessment follows:

Team Assessment

Attribute	Strongly Disagree				Neutral			Strongly Agree		
	1	2	3	4	5	6	7	8	9	10
I trust my teammates to make the right decisions about their work.										
My teammates trust me to make the right decisions about mine.										
My teammates complete their work accurately and efficiently.										
I enjoy coming to work.										
Everyone on my team has the same goal.										
My teammates are easy to get along with.										
I am able to influence how I do my job.										
My team makes it easier to do my work.										
My efforts are appreciated.										
My efforts count.										
My team is great.										
I feel like an important part of my team.										

Figure 1-1 Team Assessment Tool

The ratings tell us a lot. A five or six rating, unfortunately, means that most team members would like a different job. Many of them probably have their resumes up to date or their "feelers" out. A five or six rating also means that your team is falling behind in a world where expectations from employees, customers, and stockholders are continuing to climb. Anything below a five or six probably means imminent disaster or mutiny. Anything above a five or six means you're doing many things right, so take a bow and keep working on improvement.

Now, before you freak at the "miserable results" from your assessment, let's remember a few things. Anytime you get people together and place a manager, supervisor, or leader over them, natural dysfunctions will lead to unhappy scores. This is normal even for teams who have a leader who is highly regarded by their peers and bosses. Our culture produces the five or six team scores, and our leadership training produces the nine or 10 leader scores. Even good leadership training frequently falls short of ensuring solid connectivity with the teams, because our company and American culture are so good at interfering with it. *Our cultures are focused on the individual and not on the team.* One of the main goals of this book is to get the average scores of all team members and team leaders up to a nine or 10, by using the People Connection. If the average team score and the leader's score weren't a nine or above, then read on with anticipation.

If you're a team leader and see a high degree of misconnection and/or low team ratings, don't be discouraged. You will have lots and lots of company. It's important that you not look at low team ratings as "bad results" but simply as "what they are". Results are only bad because we call them that and then get indigestion just to make it a uniformly bad day. It's *not bad* if your team rated itself a five or six and you rated it a nine. *It just is.* You can then declare the results "good" simply by believing them to be an exciting and well-defined opportunity for improvement. This book promises to show you exactly how to take advantage of this opportunity.

Once you have mastered this different way of thinking, you should compile and analyze the results and share them with your team. It's important to master the thinking first; otherwise they will see your disappointment, which won't be good. Please resist the temptation to draw conclusions and develop solutions without talking with your team. Some solutions will seem obvious, but resisting their temptations will make you a smart and wise leader who knows enough to avoid an embarrassing trap. The team wants 10 ratings as badly as you do. If you share the results with them, and ask them what it will take to get to a 10, they will take you there.

If you see just a few unusually low scores in certain areas, pursue those as if they were valid. Sometimes, just a few people are perceptive or bold enough to identify problems that, when corrected, will improve team performance. Even if they are not valid, the fact that you gave them respectful attention shows that you care and are willing to listen, which is a big deposit for your leadership bank account. A small number of unusually low scores would suggest that you use casual, no pressure, one-on-one discussions to clarify the issues and the corrective actions required. A large number of unusually low scores, on the other hand, would suggest that you ask the team what to do about them.

CHAPTER 1 CLOSING COMMENTS

The Chinese character for crisis consists of two symbols: one meaning danger, and the other opportunity. A "bad score" crisis is an opportunity, and the danger lies in reacting to it the wrong way. Were the developers of this character thinking the same things we are right now?

∞CHAPTER 2: INFINITE POWER BEGINS HERE!

If you want to make minor, incremental changes and improvements, work on practices, behavior or attitude. But if you want to make significant, quantum improvement, work on paradigms.

– Stephen Covey

In this age of boastful, but frequently hollow claims, the People Connection delivers. In fact, it usually over delivers because of its tendency to surprise the leaders. *The People Connection has produced gains of at least 20 to 30 percent in just about every measure within three to 12 months in 10 successive organizations.* It's easy to understand, it's logical, and it's practical.

However, it's way outside of our American paradigms. Paradigms are belief systems. Paradigms are what we believe about people, processes, and business. Paradigms greatly influence how we think, what we do, and *even what we can actually see. Your paradigms could very well blind you to what I am saying for awhile; so if it's not clear yet, it will be soon.*

The People Connection has produced gains of at least 20 to 30 percent in just about every measure within three to 12 months in10 successive organizations.

Table 2-A on the following page shows the before and after states of a typical team or organization after they have experienced the change process of the People Connection.

Table 2-A. Before and after the People Connection.

The Impact of This Process on a Team	
Before	**After**
Low to medium morale	High morale
Low to medium enthusiasm and engagement	High enthusiasm and engagement
Team needs prodding and pushing to get the job done	Team regularly exceeds expectations
Team members don't get along well	Team members work very well together
Team complains of overwork	Complaints almost dissappear
Team has a huge number of problems	Problems are inconsequential and are quickly solved or brushed aside
Team needs lots of help and attention	Team can function fine by itself
Team seems to be riddled with poor performers	Poor performers disappear
Team seems to have very few high performing natural leaders	Team is full of leaders
Team members complain about one another	Complaints almost dissappear
Team members are territorial	Boundaries between team members disappear
Team members complain about the boss	Complaints almost disappear
High turnover	Turnover is almost nonexistent
Hard to get team members to change	Team members drive the change
Goals are hard to meet	Goals are routinely and significantly surpassed
Absenteeism medium to high	Absenteeism low
Team spirit is poor to so-so	Team spirit is high
Rules are hard to enforce	Team makes tougher rules that have no enforcement problems
Good ideas are hard to come by	Ideas of all kinds routinely expand the effectiveness of the team
Team members complain about the pay	Complaints almost dissappear
Team members complain about the working conditions	Complaints almost dissappear
Team members complain about the benefits	Complaints almost dissappear
Team leaders, managers, and bosses are overworked	These three simply become leaders and are enjoying their work
Many leaders, managers, and bosses need replaced	Almost all become key players

Before we proceed, I want to clarify what this book is not. It's not an attempt to detract from the value of management strategies and initiatives such as Outsourcing, Lean, or Six Sigma. "Outsourcing" is the process of contracting people outside your company who can provide your products or services less expensively or more effectively than you can. "Lean" is the removal of wasted time, materials, and other costs from your processes. "Six Sigma" is the process of removing the variation in your processes, so that rejects and customer dissatisfaction can be avoided.

Lean and Six Sigma both use teamwork and a complex set of tools to attack problems that beset all organizations. All three of these initiatives, as well as others, have tremendous value – *if the right foundation work has been completed.*

The People Connection provides the critical foundation for Lean and Six Sigma.

If you are unfamiliar with Lean and Six Sigma, don't worry for a second. You will learn all you need to know about them in this book. After you build the solid People Connection foundation, you will have no problem finding a wealth of resources regarding Lean and Six Sigma should you choose to pursue them.

The People Connection is not some new management theory that hasn't been fully tried and tested. The principles in this Process are at least 2,000 years old, so they're a bit past the fad stage.

THE FOUNDATIONS OF THE POWER

I once read of a psychology study where two different groups were issued axes and told to chop wood for one hour. One group had dull axes and the other group had sharp axes. Everyone in the sharp axe group completed the hour of chopping wood with no problem. The group with the dull axes simply could not chop for an hour, because "they couldn't see the chips fly." Their axes were too dull to produce chips. People must see results to remain engaged.

Even if the results *are* good, there could still be a serious problem. People might fail to see themselves connected with good results, either because they are too far removed from them, or because someone else is getting the credit. For example, team members frequently see CEO's and other top executives getting paid big dollars to "save the company" or "make the tough decisions". The team members interpret this as meaning what they themselves contribute has little or no value, so they disengage.

Disengagement also occurs when individuals are singled out for recognition, when, in reality, the entire team earned it. Though it's noble for management to single out and recognize a team member, significant negative side-effects can result. It discourages and disappoints everyone who contributed to the achievement and was not recognized. The people who did not receive it feel cheated and frequently see the person being recognized as a management favorite. Interestingly enough, the person who receives the recognition usually feels that it's unfair to the others. Unless there is a random selection from a pool of all those who qualify, then "employee of the month", "most valuable player", "student of the month", or "president's award" disengage more people than can be imagined. Simply knowing they qualified and that the final selection was determined by lottery prevents a lot of this disengagement.

Let's switch gears now to one of management's key frustrations with their teams. Management will hire consultants to conduct training and to lead the company in improvement programs. These improvement programs will result in spectacular improvements in the organization, but these improvements will erode over time. Managers typically blame the team's lack of discipline or lack of commitment for the degradation in performance. It's actually not the team's fault this is happening, but the leadership's.

This degradation happens because the culture has not been uniformly changed throughout the organization to support the new way of working. The "culture" is primarily an organization's way of doing things, but culture also reflects its values and beliefs. Work was done the old way for certain reasons. Many of these reasons still exist and will, therefore, ultimately drive the organization back toward the old ways. These reasons are a part of the "culture" and will not change until the culture changes.

To illustrate: getting to work, to college, or to the mall is a problem for most people because of traffic lights and congestion. The "culture" in this illustration is how people negotiate this traffic. It will also help to think of the entire city as "the organization". The traffic engineers could work with a small percentage of the commuters and add new routes to save them time. These new routes would work great for awhile, and then people would gradually begin to realize that the best place to buy gas or coffee is on the old route, so they resume the old routes with increasing regularity. The gas stations and coffee houses didn't change locations because they weren't included in the project, plus there simply wasn't enough people taking the new routes to justify moving. The result? Time savings realized in the beginning are eventually eroded, because a number of little surprises appear that were not considered important in the original project, if considered at all. It's even possible the project team deliberately did not address this problem because they didn't understand its importance, or because they were limited on manpower and/or time.

The People Connection is by far the easiest, quickest, and most efficient way to change the culture. Culture can be difficult and painful – if not impossible – to change without it. Fortunately, for late adopters of the People Connection, the culture can be changed independently of improvement projects, which means that it can be done before, during, or after the projects. The People Connection will produce significant improvements on its own, as well as create the right foundation to sustain other improvement efforts.

It's a trap to believe that group resistance to change is due to the personalities of the people doing the work. It's also incredibly easy to overlook the power and influence of culture when planning and executing a project.

Falling into this trap disengages the team. They can see what's going on; they know management is disappointed in them; they feel powerless to do anything about it – and they are. So they simply give up.

The greatest challenge that management faces in this global economy is to completely engage the workforce in the business. Failure to fully engage the workforce leads to employee dissatisfaction and substandard team performance. It also leads to the erosion of almost all conventional improvement efforts, most of which are isolated as in the preceding illustration. It can ultimately lead to organization failure. Now, let's turn to the solution.

GAINING MOMENTUM WITH THE POWER

The People Connection engages the team by directly linking them with the results and cultural change. *The team's need to be successful is so strong that giving them direct power over the results and cultural change is a powerful engagement mechanism.* Every person in the organization is involved in performance improvements and cultural change so improvement efforts are no longer limited by manpower (oh yes – "manpower" is generic, so it always means womanpower, also). So where does all this generic manpower come from?

The weekly all-staff meeting connects *all* the manpower in the organization. More than one meeting would be required if there are more than 20 people in the organization (one meeting per group per week). Once the entire organization is connected and engaged, they move forward together, and the improvements occur throughout the organization rather than in isolated areas. Because all areas work together and own the results, there is little or no significant erosion of the gains that have been made. *This meeting has a standing agenda that brings the goal into clear focus, generates ideas on how to reach that goal, and involves everyone in implementing those ideas.*

NOTE: I will use the terms "mission, goal, and vision" interchangeably from here forward, even though they are very different, because they're managed the same way in the People Connection.

It's impossible to overstate the importance of bringing the goal into clear focus. The lack of focus on the goal, or vision, is one of the most costly organizational traps there is, and the one most littered with victims. I've seen leaders hundreds of times declare that everyone shared the same goal, because it was so simple and because all team members **_said_** they understood. The vision and mission statement were carefully worded and printed in beautiful font, framed, and hung proudly on the meeting room and lobby walls for all to see. When the team doesn't perform, then *those same leaders blame the team members for their lack of commitment.*

> *The greatest challenge that management faces in this global economy is to completely engage the workforce in the business.*

This "blaming" attitude keeps a lot of teams in the ditch. When the effort is made to get the honest opinions from each team member in a situation like this, we will almost always find that there are at least two different interpretations of the goal. *These different interpretations are really different agendas,* and the result is a mix of frustrated people who can't reach the goal, confused and dazed people who can't function, and the rest who don't have a clue and mentally check out.

One Goal
+ Everyone's Ideas
+ Everyone's Efforts
= SUCCESS!

> *The weekly meeting has a standing agenda that brings the goal into very clear focus, generates ideas on how to reach that goal, and involves everyone in implementing those ideas.*

This weekly meeting prepares everyone for the more sophisticated cost and quality improvement initiatives such as Lean and Six Sigma. As introduced earlier in this chapter, Lean is a sophisticated methodology to remove wastes and costs and Six Sigma is a highly disciplined program using statistical tools to remove variation and costs. These sophisticated and powerful tools cannot be entrusted with any degree of confidence to those who aren't prepared to use them and support them. This meeting does an excellent job in preparing teams for these tools.

To prove the point, let's consider the following. Let's say you want to save money on car repairs, and your friends have told you about a garage that has the lowest labor *rates* in town. This garage has been around awhile, but all their tools are new, shiny, sophisticated, and impressive. All their long-time employees have just been "trained and certified" as mechanics and in using these new tools. Would you trust these people with your car? I wouldn't, and here's why.

I have little confidence that these mechanics can do the job correctly. There's a lot more to being a mechanic than simply knowing how to use the tools. There's a lot of judgment involved that comes from experience, practice, and especially a solid grounding in the fundamentals. Good mechanics have developed good judgment and intuition. They can read between the lines of sophisticated test equipment results, and find the *real* cause of a problem. An inexperienced mechanic could very well rely on his new tools way too much, and end up replacing many more parts for you than necessary.

Huge car maintenance bills are common horror stories, so this is not an unrealistic example. We often say mechanics are crooked; but more often than not, huge bills can very well be due to poor management rather than poor ethics. Technology is frequently given more priority and emphasis than people, so we end up with relatively low paid mechanics and high cost equipment, which as we can see is the recipe for repair robbery. Even though the labor rates may be cheaper, the bill costs more because more labor and parts were used than were necessary.

Anyone who is expected to fix things needs to understand them thoroughly first. *Understanding doesn't develop nearly as well with complex and sophisticated training as it does with guidance and experience.* The simple basics need to be thoroughly engrained first. <u>Let me say it another way: it's not a good idea to skip elementary school in anything important as our work.</u>

What the team really needs is to learn and apply the *basics* of Lean and Six Sigma for a period of time before they can be called "mechanics." It's the basics, not the tools, that will give them the true ability to improve team performance. Great tools in the hands of those with true ability are very powerful; great tools in the hands of those who simply go through the motions they were trained for will deliver only mediocre results. The weekly People Connection meeting focuses team members on mastering the basics.

UNDERSTANDING THE POWER

A team's power begins by accumulating each team member's strengths, talents, knowledge, and efforts. Great tasks can, therefore, be accomplished without straining the average team member. However, a team's power is greater than the sum of its members. To understand how this is so, let's turn to the weekly meeting.

The weekly meeting taps into a deep well of energy, enthusiasm, and commitment. Ralph Stayer from Johnsonville Foods said: "People want to be great, and they want to be a part of something great." People need a purpose. If you don't believe it, just watch and listen carefully to the world around us. The proof is everywhere. Deprive people of purpose and the means to fulfill it, and a huge list of ills we are so familiar with today quickly materializes. *Each person has a need to be significant, and the most important thing a leader can do is to make filling that need possible. When leaders do this, they will have unlocked the powerhouse that is central to the People Connection.*

Thousands of decisions get made every day that don't get approved by management, because those decisions are essentially invisible due to their overwhelming numbers. They are invisible, that is, until they make a bad impact. Decisions such as: what am I going to say to this customer? Can I get away with extending my break a little? Should I rework this part or throw it away? What difference will it make if I just fudge the data a little? If everyone on the team has a different understanding of the goal, then these decisions will drive the team in just about every different way except the way intended by the leader.

The vision or goal takes significant calendar time, frequent and creative spot checks on understanding (that don't sound repetitious), and the weekly all-staff short discussions about what the goal means to everyone. Only then can it become a truly shared goal. When the goal or vision is interpreted differently by each team member, they essentially have different agendas and that's deadly to teamwork. In many cases these differences are so subtle that only very careful attention and discernment can reveal them. Finding and correcting these differences requires a safe environment, persistence, patience, intense listening, and careful diplomacy.

Each person has a need to be significant, and the most important thing a leader can do is to make filling that need possible.

Once the goal is truly shared, then everyone has exactly the same agenda. At this point we can expect all decisions to be aimed at the goal. That's when we begin to notice the synergy in teamwork that we all love to see. Synergy is when the total is greater than the sum of the individual effects; in other words, when the team performance is greater than the collection of individual efforts. "Like-mindedness" is another term that applies to a team that truly shares a goal.

The People Connection

The Mindset

1. View the team as one individual instead of a collection of individuals.

2. Understand that people want to be great and to be a part of something great.

3. Believe that the most powerful motivator for team members is an environment where they can achieve greatness as a team.

4. Understand that *every* team or organization consists of 20 percent on the top, 20 percent on the bottom, and 60 percent in the middle.

5. Everyone, including the team leader, has blind spots and needs to rely on others to fill in those blind spots.

6. The leader's first priority is the team, not the customer.

7. The team's first priority is the customer, not the leader.

8. Understand that perseverance, integrity, humility, and staying the course are essential.

9. Understand that the rate of progress will appear glacially slow every single day; however, viewed in hindsight it will appear remarkably fast.

10. Progress will be bumpy; rapid progress will be followed by what *appears* to be regression, followed by even higher levels of achievement.

11. Don't replace people to make this Process work; let the Process take care of the bottom 20 percent.

12. Understand that the Process is just as important as the results, and that the Process requires a lot of attention.

The Meeting

1. Only three standing agenda topics for the one-hour weekly team meeting:

   a. 5 minutes — ensure vision or goal is crystal clear — this will take weeks or even months.

   b. 50 minutes — ask what it will take to reach the vision or goal.

   - The people doing the job make the best decisions about their jobs, even though it doesn't seem like it at first.

   - Unless the decisions are going to break the law, break the budget, or hurt someone, then let the team carry them out.

   - Let those with the ideas volunteer to carry them out.

   - Ensure those carrying out the improvement ideas are provided the time and other resources to carry them out.

   - Eliminate waste due to variation in the process.

   - Eliminate wasted time in the process.

   c. 5 minutes — ask what the team is doing well and what it can do better; monitor "resonance", which is how well the team is working together.

2. Preserve a brainstorming climate throughout the entire meeting; in other words, there is no such thing as a bad idea, thought, or question.

3. Disable the pecking order by using the "puzzle" analogy; each person is a piece to the puzzle and no one is more important than another.

4. Always focus on leading the 60 percent in the middle; the top 20 and bottom 20 percents can't, or won't, do much more for the team.

5. Debrief with process partner(s) after each meeting.

6. Keep minutes and records of team progress in order to help prevent the negative effects of impatience (no more than one page per meeting).

7. Promote full participation and open communications between all team members.

8. This meeting sets the tone and the example for teamwork that carries through the week.

Figure 2D: A summary of the People Connection

The journey into the People Connection is now in full-swing. Before we proceed, however, it will be useful to see the summary of this Process, which is shown in Figure 2D on page 23. Though this summary has a couple dozen line items on it, that does not mean it's complicated. As the headings show, the People Connection is simply a three-topic weekly meeting and a mindset that feels very natural after awhile. This summary should prove to be a useful reference for the rest of the book.

∞ CHAPTER 3: WHAT DOES YOUR ORGANIZATION NEED?

We must always take a careful look at what our organization really needs before beginning any kind of change initiative. The People Connection is successful because it fills people's needs *and* the organization's needs. The driving need of people is to be great and to be a part of something great. But what is the driving need of an *organization*? The following three true stories will set the stage for answering that question.

HOW THE PEOPLE CONNECTION AFFECTS ORGANIZATIONS

My first People Connection experience was with the Foams Plant in 1986. The company decided we were going to implement SPI, or Statistical Process Improvement. SPI was very similar to, but more basic, than today's Six Sigma and Lean. It also had significant elements of teamwork in it. My partner, Steve Estes, and I were responsible, as full-time employees, for training all 500 people in this facility, hourly and salaried workers alike. Though this was a corporate initiative, it was not so tightly controlled that Steve and I couldn't put a much bigger emphasis on teamwork than the other 20 facilities in our division did.

About a year after we started the initiative, we had a visitor from a major brush company. Frank Jones, their VP of Manufacturing, Steve, and I had dinner together, and then Frank spent most of the following day meeting with our hourly people, but not us. He was impressed with our people and Process and wrote us a nice letter that included this comment: "Your plant certainly walks the talk with a rating of 11 on a one-to-ten scale. The only other plant I have seen that shows the glow of pride in every employee is Honda America." We had obviously connected with our people. Either by blessing or incredible luck, we had hit on something really grand in this first experience.

Here are some other comments about the Foams Plant from Ray Greene, a consultant, and Dave Thomas, from our division's Corporate Quality Assurance Department: "If you were in the automobile industry, you would definitely be rated as a Q-1 [top rank] supplier. The overall program is farther along after one year than any other program we have ever seen. Commitment and enthusiasm at all levels of the organization are excellent." Again, people from outside the company noticed something significant going on in this plant.

This wasn't simply feel good stuff, either. The Foams Plant improved their profits by 33 percent that first year. Our financial people were stunned, because there was neither precedence nor conventional explanation for the profit increase where chronic shortfalls were the norm. They were looking for project reports that could pinpoint where the profit improvements were coming from. Our teams (about 40 of them on any given day) were spending all their time on reducing variation and waste, and spent no time on reporting, because nothing seemed big enough by itself to report. Hundreds and hundreds of tiny improvements were making a huge difference.

The second experience involves the Decatur Plant. This facility produced emergency light fixtures of every description, as well as a line of Controls products. Controls products are expensive, sophisticated devices that control lighting in theatres, auditoriums, and large buildings. Controls was not a high volume business, but because of its complexity and great number of design variations, it was a demanding business. Controls required a much higher percentage of everyone's time than the sales volumes would indicate. On-time delivery was harder to produce because of product complexity and the availability of specialized components. On-time product delivery, which we called *"service"*, was a major issue and many people were very anxious – customers, top management, sales people, and plant personnel.

This service problem was also chronic. Controls had always, at best, run about a 30 percent allocation failure rate, which is a measure of service where less is better. An allocation failure was actually an early warning system that told us we did not have the product to fill an order that we just received, even though we didn't need to ship the order for two weeks or so. All other product lines averaged about a four percent allocation failure rate.

To address this problem, we engaged everyone who had anything to do with Controls service, which included our sales and marketing people, as well as the entire group of our manufacturing people. We used the People Connection to focus everyone on the goal and on how to get there. We met regularly, week after week, everyone taking their bite-size assignment for the week, while doing their regular job. As the manager of the Decatur plant, I led this effort, but the team created the results.

We did nothing dramatic or terribly time-consuming, just a whole series of simple, seemingly inconsequential, steps that collectively made a huge difference. We immediately diffused the finger-pointing by drawing attention to the goal every time there was a problem. We focused on what it was going to take to become the best in the industry, instead of what it was going to take to fix our service problems. We contacted each of our suppliers before we placed component orders with them, just to ensure they were ready for our orders. We stopped expediting finished product orders, which was essentially making a customer happy by allowing them "to go to the head of the line". We created a separate inventory for sales service parts and a procedure for re-stocking that inventory. The list goes on and on, and within two to three months, it was clear we had made significant progress.

Ken Fletcher, the President and CEO of our company, had this to say about our progress: "Is this a misprint? Can it possibly be true that Controls now has a lower allocation failure rate than Cochran, Vermilion and Craw-fordsville [our sister manufacturing facilities]!!? I don't believe that has ever happened in the history of the company. Congratulations." To under-score Ken's comment regarding the history of the company, Controls had been an active product line for about 20 years.

Decatur's Controls product allocation failure rate was now at 3.6 per-cent, with Cochran's products at 4.5 percent, Vermilion at 5.1 percent, and Crawfordsville at 6.1 percent. With very little additional effort, Controls later set a record at just under 2.0 percent, a long ways from 30 to 50 per-cent. ***This true story demonstrates the tremendous power of the People Connection.***

The third and last experience is the Berkeley Plant shutdown. When I was called in as a consultant to review and comment on their shutdown plans, it appeared that everything was in order for a late February to late March shutdown, which was ambitious but possible. I told them they could handle it themselves with the people and the processes they were using. However, as I was walking out the door, it was brought to my at-tention that though this was mid-November, there was going to be a huge financial penalty for not having the plant totally evacuated by the end of December. This required a 60 to 70 percent reduction in the shutdown process timeline. At that moment, I recommended that we use a different process, and we started work immediately.

The Berkeley Plant's workforce bordered on hostile, since the shut-down schedules had been delayed too many times, and because their jobs would come to an end when the shutdown finally occurred. Morale and housekeeping were poor. Attitudes toward the company and management were sour. The receiving plants were not in the best shape to receive the products, either. It simply was a bad situation all around for an accelerated shut-down plan. We quickly implemented the People Connection and this is what happened:

The story is best told by what the acting plant manager told me on December 29, two days before we were supposed to be out of the facility. I was not there because of family obligations, and because I had faith that the team could get this job done without my actual presence. I phoned Ken Mathis, the acting plant manager, to ask how it was going. He said, "All production will be complete today. All remaining components will be shipped today. Morale is the highest I have seen it for a long, long time. The work is hard, but you know what, it's actually fun." Remember that this comment was about a plant full of people who would be out of work the next day. When people are achieving a goal and can show that they are great, that feeling over-rides problems like loss of jobs. These people understood for years that the plant would shut down and it was actually a relief for them that it finally happened. The People Connection made this possible.

There are more stories like this, but they all have this in common, the People Connection is enormously effective *in all kinds* of situations. It will improve morale, service, quality, productivity, and just about anything else that involves people and processes.

These experiences are not freaks. I have discovered many people, books, and articles in my 22 years of study, who have related successes with processes similar to the People Connection. The People Connection has benefited significantly from these resources, as well as the intense experiences related in this book. As a result, the People Connection has in many ways surpassed them all in simplicity and effectiveness. The crucial point here, however, is that *collectively, the experiences of many other successful practitioners, in essence, validates the People Connection.*

WHERE TO START IF YOUR ORGANIZATION NEEDS REPAIRS

Repairing a malfunctioning organization is actually easier than improving a good one – until the momentum builds, and then they're the same. In a repair situation, most team members are already aware, at least to some degree, that things aren't right. They are as anxious as the leaders to get them resolved. Frustrations already permeate the organization. People gripe about top management and their boss.

For many years, I actually believed it was tougher turning around a broken organization than running one that was already working well. Since I had spent so many years in challenging turn-around and shut-down situations, I was looking forward to the day when our team, any one of them, finally "arrived". When that day finally came, I was at a loss. I was afraid I would not be able to keep my team out of the dreaded swamp of complacency. I actually began to miss the urgent problems I was so used to. I finally realized that *teams always work better when they face challenges far beyond their comfort zone, if not the struggle for survival, then some other kind of crisis.*

There are some serious traps in crises, however. Team members badly want relief from the daily grind of problems and frustrations, most of which seem easy to solve – to them. Though that is often true, one common trap is to believe that *management* needs to solve the problems. Unfortunately, management usually *lacks* all the information necessary to solve the problems satisfactorily. When they do solve them, the situation is frequently just as bad or worse. So the trap catches the team members first, management second. This is not a criticism of management, since it's not fair or even logical to expect them to solve problems when they don't have all the necessary information.

To make things worse, solving problems is a poor strategy for making an organization more effective. Doing the right things to achieve the goal works far better than solving problems. Focusing on problems is another serious trap. Many problems will disappear (or won't matter any more) when everyone is focused on the goal. Problems multiply in a malfunctioning organization, especially when everyone focuses on them, but only a small percentage of these are key. Solve the key problems, and a large portion of the rest will be solved, too. The remainder are of so little consequence that they will get lost or forgotten in the rush to the goal.

Repairing an organization works far better if team members are empowered to do the right things to reach the goal, which includes solving some key problems that are now seen as opportunities. This gives them the chance to feel more ownership and control of their jobs as well. This ownership creates more commitment and requires more energy and thought, which team members are happy to contribute. The higher demands this Process places on people has the surprising effect of energizing, rather than draining, those doing the work.

Team members sense the opportunity to be great when they are confident in the direction their organization is moving. They sense this positive direction, and resonate with it, well before top managers can see the results that build *their own* confidence. *Team members are naturally far more sensitive to the forward momentum of the organization than management is.*

> *Solving problems is a poor strategy for making an organization more effective. Doing the right things to achieve the goal works far better than solving problems.*

For many people, especially the leaders, the People Connection has all the speed sensation of a glacier when viewed in the impatient and frantic present, although it's obviously fast when seen in the rear view mirror. People from outside the organization can easily see the progress also. No one should be concerned about the lack of breakthrough improvements. The fact is there are more than enough small change opportunities that, collectively, will produce 20 to 30 percent improvements in a short time.

> *Team members are far more sensitive to the forward momentum of the organization than management is.*

WHERE TO START IF YOU WANT TO MAKE A GOOD ORGANIZATION GREAT

In his best selling book <u>Good to Great</u>[4], Jim Collins makes the point that one of the greatest obstacles to a company's becoming great is that it's already good. There's nothing like being the underdog, or being in a crisis to energize people. Being good creates complacency, not fanatical drive. Jim Collins is a best-selling author who is a student of enduring great companies. His research team of 20 people invested about 15,000 hours in developing <u>Good to Great.</u>

Leaders in a good organization will need to create a crisis if they intend to significantly improve performance. We need to look deep inside our business strategy and business environment to see if there's a potential crisis that can be addressed now. Even if no crisis can be found, we still need to create a *highly* challenging vision, or a goal, that will – or can – excite our team. *Realism is not a virtue here.* Visions that initially seem impossible to the team or organization can be the best.

Even as we stretch ourselves to this extreme, we still have to balance this craziness with reality by looking hard at our team and asking ourselves what fits them best. What's their passion? What are they best at? How can they make money? The answers these three questions have in common are the ones we're looking for. One of these needs to be elevated to vision status and then we proceed full-speed ahead with the People Connection.

THE ORGANIZATION'S MOST IMPORTANT NEED

Managers, leaders, and stockholders, let's talk philosophically for just a moment.

People are not only our greatest asset; they are our organizations' reason for existence. Hang on; I gave us time to be friends before I said something so bold, so please bear with me. I understand this is a radical statement, but I think it's necessary to accept this concept in order to make an organization truly great.

Think about it. They wouldn't be in your organization if they didn't need a job. *Customers become number one only after your people make them that way. If you are a leader, your organization or team is number one. To your organization or team, the customer is number one.*

Connecting with your people in the most effective and efficient manner possible is, therefore, your first priority. You must know who they are, what excites them, and how to engage them to their limits. They really do want full engagement and all the discipline and commitment that requires. Don't forget, they are looking for a leader first, friend second. Getting to know them on a personal basis is no substitute for filling their need to be great. Keep your team number one and they will ensure that your customers are number one.

The People Connection will do many things for you. Your people won't look for the path of least resistance, when they see a challenge that will fulfill them. They won't look for someone to solve their problems, when they feel the empowerment to work towards a shared goal that is exciting. They will encourage and engage other team members to work towards the goal, rather than expect management to do it. The more that management empowers them, the more responsibility they are willing to take on themselves.

A word of caution, however, before you launch this initiative in your organization or team. Though this Process is extremely simple and proven many times over in many organizations, it's not necessarily easy to implement. It requires the right mindset that may take some time to adjust to in the beginning. Many different programs have been followed in pursuing extraordinary results, and those paths are littered with failures. The People Connection – though it provides by far the greatest chance of success – can also fail if we don't make the full paradigm shift necessary to make it work.

Let's take a quick look at some sobering statistics so we don't look naïve as we work to master this Process.

> *People are not only our greatest asset; they are our organizations' reason for existence.*

∞CHAPTER 4: WHAT IS THE PROBABILITY OF SUCCESS?

Quite frankly, 95 percent (frequently quoted in business magazines) of improvement programs and plans don't fulfill top management's expectations. General Motors, Ford, Chrysler, and many others have attempted and ultimately been disappointed with celebrity leaders, Lean, Six Sigma and other improvement programs.

Jim Collins, in his book <u>Good to Great</u>, discovered in his thorough and praiseworthy research that factors such as "Level 5 Leaders, having the right people on the bus, and staying the course" are keys to success[5]. *<u>He also discovered that improvement programs were not a factor in creating greatness.</u>* Contrary to Collins' finding, companies continue to depend on improvement programs, while overlooking the essential ingredient of success – their people. The People Connection, as a point of clarification, is not a program; it's a mindset and a process.

On the other hand, five percent who try do very well. How did Toyota, Honda, and others succeed? Even though much of the record is now buried in time, what worked decades ago still works today. Leadership, people, and staying a course that many perceive to be "too simple" to be effective are what really make the difference. Toyota teaches Lean today, but their grandfathers are the ones who had to learn it from Dr. W. Edwards Deming and Henry Ford after World War II. Dr. Deming was an American quality improvement guru who most U.S. companies ignored – until Japan surfaced as an economic powerhouse due to his leadership. The Japanese felt they had to listen to Dr. Deming, because their survival was at stake. Nobody wanted to buy the junk they were making right after WWII, and they had to have overseas customers to survive. They didn't have the natural resources to survive in isolation. Survival crises set the stage for the success of Toyota, Honda, the Foams Plant, the Decatur Plant (chapter 2) and many others like them.

The Japanese of a couple of generations ago learned their lessons so well and engrained them so deeply they became a part of their organizational DNA (their genes). And perhaps their grandsons are underselling their key strength, because the "Toyota Way" is seen by Americans today as "Lean" rather than as people and leadership. In other words, Americans are giving the tools more emphasis and attention rather than the leadership mindset that made Toyota's Lean methodology so successful. Remember the mechanic analogy from chapter 2? Great mechanics can produce great results even with modest tools, whereas great tools in the hands of underdeveloped mechanics will produce only mediocre results. It is imperative that leaders develop great "mechanics" *before* they employ powerful improvement tools. Careful examination will show that successful Japanese companies still place the highest value on their people.

American companies have a strong affinity for the methodology side of the formula, which is Lean, but they have much more difficulty with the people side of it, which is the "soft stuff". Tom Malone of the award-winning Milliken Company told an audience, "It's the soft stuff that is the hard stuff, but it's the soft stuff that makes the difference." People are the soft stuff: hard to define, hard to measure, hard to understand, and therefore hard to manage and manipulate. Financial reports, programs, improvement initiatives, and projects are much easier to control and measure, much neater, and much more convenient. The challenge, therefore, rests with how to become successful in leading and working with people.

To better understand Toyota and others from Japan who are consummate experts of Lean, please reflect on the following from the book **Gemba Kaizen** by Masaaki Imai. Mr. Imai is considered one of the leaders of the quality movement. He is also an international lecturer, consultant, and chairman of the Kaizen Institute of Japan. Mr. Imai says:

"Workers must be inspired to fulfill their roles, to feel proud of their jobs, and to appreciate the contribution they make to their company and society. Instilling a sense of mission and pride is an integral part of management's responsibility…"[6]

This approach to team members and leadership is essentially the same as the People Connection. The People Connection inspires the people doing the job by engaging them, challenging them, and encouraging them. They gain a sense of pride from improving their work themselves. They (and management) can appreciate their contributions more by seeing how their efforts are reflected in improved team performance. The People Connection's focus on vision fulfills management's responsibility to instill a sense of mission. It's clear that the People Connection is consistent with Mr. Imai's philosophy.

My personal experience in using the People Connection has been 100 percent successful (10 organizations) over the past 22 years. That's not because I'm especially gifted as a leader. It's because the People Connection, in its unique way, uses timeless and proven principles that resonate powerfully with teams.

∞ CHAPTER 5: WHAT SUCCESS LOOKS LIKE

THE BIG PICTURE

Every organization that uses the People Connection has many experiences in common. The journey always seems slow – but only to those living in it. In the beginning, people won't appear to understand the Process, but will work hard and enthusiastically anyway. Many will think the vision is overemphasized. However, time quickly reveals many misunderstandings about it. Even a fast group can take months to fully clarify a common vision.

The People Connection is a lot like pushing a boulder up a hill. Day after day the leader pushes away for what seems an eternity, encountering doubt after doubt along the way. But one day, the boulder reaches the top of the hill, and that tipping point feels like it appeared out of nowhere. The tipping point is so distinct that it can usually be pinpointed to the day. Now, all of a sudden, the boulder is barreling down the other side of the hill, constantly gaining speed.

Leaders now have a new challenge. After all that patient work with the basics, they now must run hurriedly out in front of the team on the downhill side. They need to be quick and agile about removing obstacles and steering the team.

Leaders see their team in a new light. They no longer see them as a group of individuals who need personalized development and coordination. They now see them as one team with a distinct personality that needs nurturing, guidance, and challenges just as an individual would. Individuals do not suffer from this shift in focus, but instead grow more quickly through full engagement than through formal training.

Tom Peters, one of America's leading experts on organizational improvement, once said: *"The team itself will develop more rules and tougher rules*. High performing organizations are highly disciplined ones."

Team members will expect more of each other and themselves than managers normally expect of them in traditional organizations. Individuals will experience more pressure to perform because they don't want to let the team down; but they prefer this pressure to that imposed by the boss. Team accountability is more effective because individual performance, both good and bad, is more visible to teammates than to a boss, because team members work side-by-side.

The team will experience more satisfaction and less frustration because they have more control over their work. They will even show more excitement about coming to work, particularly when it involves a team activity or meeting.

The leader is challenged by the team more, which is a good thing. It means the team is beginning to think on its own, to develop its own ideas, and to learn more than ever before. Though it doesn't feel like it at first, respect grows for leaders who are not afraid of embracing the People Connection.

Leaders are frequently baffled by the team's decisions. As long as the team is following the Process, there's no need to worry. They are making decisions that are directed at the goal the leader has so patiently helped them understand. The leader does not have all the information the team does, and this information is what heavily influences their decisions. If the Process is allowed to work, then the leader will see the wisdom of the team's decisions in hindsight.

A dramatic example of this occurred when I facilitated a problem-solving meeting between a number of operators, maintenance men, and supervisors. I was an engineer at that time and had been working for years on the problem. As a matter of fact, two other engineers were working on this same problem. All the engineers stayed quiet about it because our designs would have created a lot of unwelcome ridicule. The designs had to be radical to solve an engineering problem this tough – which made them frighteningly close to being ridiculous.

The team thoroughly addressed the problem in the meeting and was ready to brainstorm solutions. We were going around the table gathering each person's ideas and I was the last one. There were no ideas left – except for my radical expandable forming drum idea. An expandable drum was designed to automatically grow and shrink the width of polystyrene foam sheet while it was still very hot and soft. Polystyrene forming drums normally had to be built with very thick aluminum walls incorporating water cooling channels and surface-coated with brittle ceramic to prevent sticking. It's impossible to grow and shrink a drum like this without being radical.

I had taught each person in this meeting that there was no such thing as a bad idea, and there was nothing else I could think of except for – an *EXPANDABLE DRUM!* I fully expected to be buried under a heap of ridicule when I finally screwed up the courage to announce that I was going to prove I practice what I preach and give them the baddest of the bad ideas.

As soon as the expandable drum idea was out of my mouth, I heard a chorus of people saying it was a ***good idea***. I was sure they misunderstood me, even as they emphasized how that would make all of their jobs so much easier and safer as well as save the company a lot of money. I quickly countered with why it couldn't work. Then suddenly, one quiet and thoughtful operator spoke up and said *I was wrong – that it would work*. When I asked him to explain himself, he pointed out that when operators were pulling the hot plastic around these drums, there was enough give in the plastic that the engineer's concern about sealing the drum was overestimated. We engineers only watched this operation from the floor, so we could not sense exactly what they were working with in a very confined space six feet above us. We could only imagine, and we were all wrong. The crucial piece of information that the engineers needed was held by the operators who had to work with this equipment.

Though I was elated that we now had a solution, I was astonished at what came next. We then took a fresh look at the drum design based on what they *really* needed and came up with a much better and less expensive design! Let's think about this for a minute. *In two hours, **one team of people, with all the relevant information, outperformed three engineers working three years.*** Engineers can do marvelous things, but there's nothing like a team of the right people to blow through the limits.

The first important lesson from this incident is that the people doing the work have critical pieces of information that no one else has access to, much less has an understanding of. *The proper environment has to exist before this information can be shared well enough to benefit the team. The second lesson is that some of the greatest ideas can come out of the worst.* It's not wise to discourage any idea if the worst can lead to the best, as it did in this case. Teams can be trusted to make superior decisions even if they appear crazy at first.

Early successes, even very small ones, will provide fuel for the team to gain momentum. Success will build enthusiasm and more success. This growing cycle accumulates into growing team performance very quickly.

This pretty well sums up what you can expect to see in your organization when you implement the People Connection. Every organization's experience is unique, although what I have just described is common to all of them. The following synopses will give you an idea of how the People Connection has helped a number of organizations.

THE FOAMS PLANT

The Foams Plant is where we began this journey in blissful ignorance. We had a handful of unlikely leaders committed to the SPI (Statistical Process Improvement) program, which our boss told us was a good thing. Our boss gave a lot of latitude to my team-mate Steve and me, and we worked very well together. We moved forward in mutual respect, energy, and enthusiasm, and fortunately agreed on the three most critical decisions for our success. These were, one, to keep the focus simple; two, don't change the process; and three, give teamwork all the support and emphasis we could muster. We didn't worry much about the methodology. We were just beginners, but we made an incredible amount of progress and improved profits by 33 percent in the very first year. This was sheer beginner's luck.

THE POLYETHYLENE PLANT

The Polyethylene Plant was my second experience with the People Connection. It was in the same plastics company as the Foams Plant. This plant had, just a short time before, declared the SPI program a failure. Surprisingly, the workforce quickly and readily embraced the second attempt of SPI, which resulted in the same kind of success we had with the Foams Plant. It was still SPI to us because we didn't realize that we were really implementing the People Connection. We were able to dramatically improve efficiencies in our reclaim area (scrap product recycling) by 15 percent in just 30 days. We accomplished this by teaching the operators how to *think as a team.* We were also highly commended by the Armstrong Corporation, a ceiling tile manufacturer that was also a Malcolm Baldrige finalist because of their world class quality program. The Malcolm Baldrige Award is given to only those few companies that exemplify outstanding commitment and results in quality.

THE CONYERS PLANT

The Conyers Plant had been a troubled plant for many years, and had gone through several years of downsizing as its products were transferred to other company facilities. Bad relations between the union and management were chronic and festering when our new leadership team arrived. We finally met our goal of matching the productivity of the other facilities;

but it was a few months past the deadline, unfortunately, so the plant was shut down. Over the course of about two years we agreed on a totally new contract, reassigned and trained everyone for their new jobs, improved productivity by 50 percent, decreased quality costs by over 90 percent, and eliminated grievances and bad union-management relations. Though the plant met a sad end, the fact was, we literally turned it upside-down and improved union-management relations to almost textbook perfection. We accomplished all of this in a timeframe that was extremely ambitious and departed this facility with our heads held high.

THE WEST COAST PLANT

The West Coast Plant was also struggling. Component inventory accuracy was getting worse every day, and production efficiencies were plummeting with them. The management team had tried all the standard solutions to no avail. We used the People Connection to put together an inventory remediation process, and improved inventory accuracy from 70 percent to the mid-90's in a month. Just about the time inventory accuracy was corrected, my boss was fired, and I was named plant manager. Within about three months, the People Connection improved productivity by 25 percent. The plant was humming again and morale was way up.

THE DECATUR PLANT

The Decatur Plant was another plant deep in serious difficulties. Service was bad; productivity and morale were low. Efficiencies improved by 30 percent in about three months. Controls, one of the major product groups, experienced service improvements (on-time product delivery) of about 95 percent. Morale skyrocketed as well. We aimed to make our plant the best place in the world to assemble emergency and controls products; and *we proved it!*

CONYERS CHURCH

The pastor of the Conyers Church told me one day that his church was dying, because the congregation did not care and was not willing to commit themselves to its work. I explained the People Connection to him and how it could help. His response was typical. He couldn't see how something so simple could do what I said it could do. The pastor finally decided to try it and soon the church took off. People became involved and enthusiastic. They clearly saw where the church was going and became instrumental in getting it there. Their responses to surveys, implementation of new ideas, support of the budget, and working in small groups broke all the records and astounded the pastor and everyone else. The Conyers Church experience taught me the People Connection is not constrained to manufacturing.

THE DECATUR PLANT OUTSOURCING PROJECT

All of the Decatur Plant's products were outsourced to three different companies in China, two in the U.S., one in Mexico, and the rest to one of our sister facilities in the U.S. Outsourcing the entire Decatur facility with sales dollars exceeding $100 million was monumental. We had about 25,000 different products to transfer and had less than two years to do it. We were promised a full-time staff of seven engineers to assist us, but those were cut from the budget before they did any work. The job rested squarely on the shoulders of the staffs of the Decatur Plant and of the receiving companies – *no extra help*. Our research has not revealed any outsourcing project of this scale anywhere else. Our team not only accomplished the goal; we did it without sacrificing service, and we did it within the prescribed time frame. This project would have failed without the People Connection.

ALABAMA PLANT

The Alabama Plant was one of the companies to which we outsourced the Decatur facility. After we had passed the point of no return in the outsourcing project, we discovered the Alabama Plant was in trouble. We could not return this product to our own facility because it was shutdown and the equipment was gone. The product transfer unexpectedly overloaded all of their systems and the resulting part shortages created the beginnings of an enormous disaster. One of my bosses, Greg Harrison, the VP of Manufacturing Transformation, and I determined that it would take about a year and a half for them to recover. Our business simply could not wait that long, so I decided to take a chance with the People Connection. In retrospect, it really didn't seem to fit this situation, but my desperation to do something – anything – impaired my thinking…fortunately. It only took the plant about a month to fully engage, and when they did, they quickly reached the tipping point. *Instead of taking a year and a half, the plant was declared recovered in just two months by my company's management!* The Alabama people, as well as the people in all of these examples, worked very hard to get these results, but they could not have succeeded without the People Connection.

BERKELEY PLANT

I deplore plant shutdowns, but the Berkeley Plant was another one I needed to do. The People Connection is full of surprises, but it seemed to outdo itself on this one. We actually got all parts, production, and people out of this facility two days ahead of a dramatically compressed plant shut-down schedule. We even added about three more weeks of production to an already crowded schedule, and completed it on the very last day of occupancy. Anyone who is familiar with moving even a household knows there is always about three times as much work as expected, so to cut

60 to 70 percent out of the move schedule is phenomenal. What is most noteworthy, however, is the fact that morale was higher in the days leading up to the plant closure than it had been for years. *The People Connection is embraced even by people who are losing their jobs.*

INSURANCE AGENCY

Scott Thurlow has one of the largest insurance agencies in the country with approximately 18 full-time employees and about 6 part-time. The insurance industry suffers from intense competitive pressures the same as many others, and Scott began noticing some serious and typical negative effects of these pressures on his organization. Productivity was slipping, morale was low, customer complaints were disturbingly high, and his people felt overworked and stressed out. To make matters worse, lack of profitability was forcing him to consider laying some people off.

We looked at his long list of problems and decided we didn't stand a chance if we tackled them head-on. His team was already overworked. We then decided to use the People Connection to get everyone focused on the same vision and working on the small weekly steps to achieve that vision. The results were remarkable. His competitive ranking in the company shot from about 80 to number 14 in less than a year. Morale is very high and lay-offs are out of the picture. Complaints of overwork and overstress have disappeared. Systems, processes and the business are better than they have been in years. Customer complaints declined from about 110 per month to one per month (yes, only *one*) in less than four months – *and no one discussed complaints or worked on them.* There seems to be no limit to what the People Connection can do for a team.

∞CHAPTER 6: WHAT HAPPENED TO OUR IMPROVEMENTS?

IMPROVEMENTS DEGRADE IF THE CULTURE DOESN'T CHANGE

It's easy and common to blame degraded results on the people doing the work. It has often been said that "they have been given all the training and support they need to adopt the new improvements, and they just won't support them." If we actually think that, don't we know deep down that's not entirely true? We leaders probably don't feel we should take the blame, because it's so hard to see where we're falling short. Furthermore, taking blame isn't high on anyone's list.

Suppose we blame it all on habit. That would only be a tad more generous than blaming it on the people. It's a persuasive argument that things go back to the old ways because old habits are hard to break. We know deep down this isn't entirely true either, even with some evidence to support it. We usually associate habits with individuals, but associating them with groups of people is usually wrong.

Most improvements start degrading almost from the day the projects are completed. If you recall the example of the new driving routes from chapter 2, unless everyone who is affected by the project is involved in it, the improvements will degrade. The gas stations and coffee houses were not involved in the project, so they didn't relocate to support the new routes. That caused people to switch back to the old routes whenever they needed their favorite gas or coffee. Not involving the entire organization in change is a common mistake and contributes far more to backsliding than old habits do. New personal habits die because of inattention or laziness. Applying these descriptions to a team is an inaccurate over-simplification.

Whether the improvements came about through a project such as a new software installation or office reorganization, the people who participate – at any level – understand and accept them better. Understanding increases buy-in, or acceptance of improvements and decisions. Note that "buy-in" means understanding and support, not a vote. If I, as a team member, buy-into a decision, it means I understand why we are doing it and how I need to support it, even if I wouldn't have voted for it. If team members were participants in an improvement project, such as a Kaizen (Japanese term for a structured days-long improvement project), then they've already bought in. Weekly all-staff meetings are great for increasing buy-in, which in turn facilitates cultural change.

Another cause of degradation, and resistance to change, is when the group's vision isn't shared. For example, two team members can agree that the vision of their organization is to win the company trophy. However, one may see the vision as working hard to make the numbers that will win the trophy, and the other may see it as improving the process that will deliver the numbers. These differences in buy-in will result in lower team performance because they lead to approaches that will clash.

TYPICAL IMPROVEMENT STRATEGIES ARE BLOODY, AND WE'RE PROUD OF IT!

As a culture we believe that change is not easy, and the pain that comes from it is a virtue. Change does require effort, stress and strain, and many times creates a sense of loss and bewilderment. It can keep us awake at night because of all of its uncertainty. People's self-worth often depends on their jobs and, therefore, change is even more difficult when it threatens their job security.

When job content and reporting relationships change, power bases are often swept away, and many managers or supervisors shift into a reactionary or a fear-based mode. Non-supervisory people also switch to this "look-out-for-number-one" mode of thinking. Team work diminishes; turnover increases;

and chaos sets in. People begin making decisions based on their own job fears and protecting their status instead of doing what is good for the team.

People become stressed to the point that they are unable to see the benefits of the change – they have tuned it out. The improvement efforts yet again encounter that old and familiar enemy called "resistance to change".

Determined change agents, however, "heroically" push through this resistance despite the human cost. Honors and accolades are often heaped upon their courageous accomplishments. However, there is usually more damage done by these "heroic" endeavors than there is benefit, and carefully constructed reports show only the rosy side of the picture. For example, huge lay-offs due to restructurings are typically followed by mediocre company performance – even though the company trumpets how much they saved in salary expenses. Claim the victory, ignore the human costs, and get the bonus. People are expendable…unnecessary costs. We actually praise and admire managers who do this! Most company downsizings and restructurings are not successful in the long run. Take some time and study the statistics, not just the exceptions and you'll see.

So why conduct change this way when there is a far better, more effective way? Using the military analogy once more, who would you bet on – the well-organized army with a rigid chain of command, or the empowered, highly trained, well-equipped and highly motivated guerrilla fighters who oppose them? I think world events have made the choice obvious, and similarly the People Connection gives the teams and organizations going through change the very clear advantage. Change is best managed by the "guerrillas" of the People Connection, even though that may disappoint those who aspire to medals and those who worship heroes and celebrities.

CULTURAL CHANGE WORKS BEST FROM THE INSIDE OUT

People are remarkably tough and resilient, especially when they are working together as a team. The team can be a formidable ally for a leader faced with difficult and even distasteful decisions. If a team or organization is facing a dire situation, it's better to get them involved right from the beginning. I have seen them handle the threat of plant closures and even real closures with remarkable calmness, fortitude, positive attitudes, and even high morale. ***Teams should never be underestimated.***

Each team has a personality of its own, and cannot be judged by the weaknesses, shortcomings, and personalities of its more notorious members. I have seen too many leaders characterize their entire teams by the personalities of a few bad eggs. Do this and the whole team suddenly becomes a bunch of bad eggs. The team can be a huge asset to a leader if it is treated as a very capable partner. They can deal with any threat and any challenge the leaders can.

A word of caution, however; focusing the team on the ***threat*** of change is not healthy. Focusing the team on the ***vision*** for countering this threat is far better. One worried leader once asked me for a list of his team's problems so we could begin fixing them. My response was that his list was overwhelming and not worth all the time and effort required to solve them. We instead focused on the vision and his team made dramatic progress. Focusing on the threat or the problem is very bad, because of the time wasted working on the wrong things. Teams usually get more of what they focus on. Focusing on the vision reduces the threat to just another step on the way to achieving that vision.

As an example, let's say that the organization's labor costs are very high, and sales are declining due to foreign competition. Rather than follow the example of others and begin outsourcing, why not present the problem to the team? The vision could be to become the world leader in their market, and the team could be empowered to implement the thousands of small steps to get there. Collectively, these ideas normally produce across the board improvements of 20 to 30 percent very quickly. This may be enough to achieve the vision. If not, there is now a solid foundation for implementing Lean and/or Six Sigma, which are proven programs for significantly improving organization performance.

At least one plant was closed because this advice was not followed. This plant was working toward a goal of being the best place in the world to produce their particular products. However, the siren song of low Chinese labor rates and the outsourcing fad was too much for top management to resist. They closed the facility and within a year or two realized the plant really was the best at what they were doing. Almost 300 people lost their jobs for the wrong reasons, and the company also suffered. The team usually wants the same things top management does, and the results are often tragic when they are not made partners in the change process.

If the performance gap still cannot be closed, at least the workforce will more fully understand the situation and will appreciate being given a fair chance at solving the problem. This understanding leads to a calmer and more mature acceptance of the situation. It also leads to greater cooperation in all of the things that must be accomplished while going through the necessary changes. For example, management may need excellent cooperation in properly transferring equipment, components, and training so the time and effort invested in making the team a partner will reap excellent returns.

I believe people are designed for change and are invigorated by it. Normal resistance to change is largely a conditioned reaction to bad or poorly managed change processes. People go through physical, emotional, and spiritual changes their entire lives, and they are designed for it. They are actually invigorated by change when they successfully meet its challenges and discover its benefits. Changes such as marriage, the first baby, the first job, and a promotion are often met with fear and trepidation, which are soon overshadowed by excitement and promise.

I also believe people desire change. They get tired of the same old thing after awhile and want something different. Just look at how eager people are to change the same old problems they face day after day. If all change could be initiated and controlled by those going through it, then there would probably be a whole lot more enthusiasm for change. Of course, that is not always realistic. However, a wise leader can certainly leverage this desire and need for change by using the People Connection.

The People Connection is a powerful tool to use for communicating and understanding the need for change, properly designing it, and then smoothly and efficiently implementing it. It harmonizes with people's propensity for change instead of conflicting with it. Change should not be forced on people in a top-down style, because it is usually resented and inefficient, if not totally ineffective. The change process can actually be improved by using the People Connection. Yes, improved – *when a threat or challenge is addressed from within the team, rather than imposing it on the team, the outcomes are almost always far better than can be imagined in the beginning.*

LEARNING AND PRACTICING
THE PROCESS

This is the second of three sections in this book. Congratulations on reading this far. You must be really interested in contributing to your team's success. The readers who truly want to give 100 percent as either a team member or leader should complete this section and the next. Good teamwork doesn't take a lot of effort; it just takes the right effort.

This section is at a higher level than the preceding section. I assure you there will be plenty of oxygen as we climb.

The goal of this section is to teach you how to practice the People Connection. The third section teaches how to understand and master the process. Mastering the process is what really makes it come alive in a way you never thought possible. After twenty plus years of it, I never cease to be amazed. I think you will be, too.

∞CHAPTER 7: LOOKING DEEP INTO THE PROCESS

"The very essence of leadership is (that) you have a vision. It's got to be a vision you articulate clearly and forcefully on every occasion. You can't blow an uncertain trumpet."

– Theodore Hesburgh

IT REALLY IS THIS SIMPLE – THE DECATUR PLANT STORY

Let's revisit the Decatur plant because it's so rich in learning experiences.

Decatur was a premier plant for many years, but had fallen on hard times sometime before I arrived. Due to circumstances beyond their direct control they were short-staffed, service was chronically poor, and morale was low. I was asked to take the assignment as plant manager and fix the situation.

We promptly switched to a different approach. I was very open in explaining how much trouble we were in, but assured them we could recover if we just focused on becoming the best manufacturer of our products in the world.

Things started to shape up rapidly as all those little contributions from each team member added up. We quickly added the staff we needed to function and thrive. We attacked service issues aggressively. The Controls product line had the worst service, so we set up a team to address it. The Controls story was told earlier, but was only a small part of the Decatur story. The plant had very little time to spend on recovery, but the People

Connection was so efficient and effective that not much time was actually required.

Perseverance was key. The vision was constantly repeated, and the team quickly became engaged in reaching it. There were conflicts and confusion, but refocusing was quick and easy. We simply repeated the questions: where are we going and what's it going to take to get there? Personal agendas disappeared and people focused on reaching the goal.

It soon became apparent that one critical need, a reliable component supply, was not something the plant team was going to be able to fulfill. A recent company organization change created a part shortage problem for us that we could not totally resolve. The company had decided to centralize into functional silos and the relationships between these silos were not properly aligned for Decatur's unique needs. Functional silos are areas like finance, engineering, and marketing, which focus on optimizing their own performance and not necessarily the performance of the entire organization. Decatur had to source their parts from the volatile electronic component markets. Though the people in these silos are doing what they are expected to do, they can frequently find themselves giving priority to their silo's goals instead of the organization's goals whenever conflicts between the two occur.

Central Sourcing was responsible for the sourcing of components for all plants, which included selecting the supplier and agreeing on the price. Central Sourcing's process focused on price, and was ineffective at giving sufficient weight to supplier service and quality, which were critical to a plant's performance. Top management felt that the plant was responsible for service, and Central Sourcing was responsible for price. Central Sourcing got credit for saving a lot of money. However, this arrangement didn't work for the plant, because the suppliers knew that only Central Sourcing could "fire" them, and as long as their prices were right, they could get away with substandard service and quality. The plant tried repeatedly to resolve this issue but could not. To survive, therefore, Decatur had to be very creative. The People Connection was a perfect tool for tapping the creativity of the Decatur team.

Relentless improvements, as well as creativity, were also critical. The Controls story told earlier is probably the best illustration of Decatur's creativity, focus, and perseverance, because it's the easiest to explain. Even so, it was the most challenging because of the complex nature of the product and the market. The Controls challenge connected our Marketing, Engineering, Production, Scheduling and Buying/Planning functions into an effective and efficient team.

"Controls service is in the ditch, and it's all manufacturing's fault" was something we heard at least daily in the weeks after I arrived in Decatur. We needed a recovery plan and we needed it quickly. We approached the production and buying/planning people. We listened to all their concerns regarding parts delivery problems, and how some of these part shortages were due to field service representatives taking them without permission. We listened to the scheduling people, and heard that when service worsened, it was aggravated by speeding up some customer orders which caused delays for others. The picture we got from these discussions is that it wasn't as simple as blaming manufacturing for all of the problems. It was clear we needed the PMD's (Product and Market Development) help.

After some fairly stiff resistance from PMD management to getting involved, we were finally able to get Steve Kauffman's help. Steve was the Director of Controls for the PMD. Steve and I brought all of our key Controls PMD and manufacturing people together. Our scheduler Tracy Newsom, buyer/planner Joey Davison, PMD order coordinator Kellie Watson and the rest of the team began by identifying our vision. Our goal was to be the best in the Controls market, not simply to fix our current service problems. We then did an assessment of our current situation. Steve was receiving about 10 customer complaints per day. Within 4 months of starting this process, he was getting about 1 per week, and new production records were being set on a regular basis. That year was a record sales year.

We never focused on the problems; we focused on how we were going to be the best in the market. That relieved us of the time-consuming burden of analyzing all of our problems, and then identifying and implementing corrective actions. We had insufficient manpower to employ conventional methodology.

 This cross-functional team quickly began to think differently. They stopped looking at their jobs as being in separate "silos", and instead began to see how each of their activities related to those in other functional areas. Action plans began to look cross-functional, and the distinctions between team members' jobs blurred. Though this behavior is well-known, it usually isn't practiced. The People Connection is an easy way to create cross-functional teamwork.

Controls service achieved record levels, and it required very little additional effort. The following charts, Figures 7A and 7B, track this remarkable journey. Please note the lasting effect of this changed way of thinking, since these charts cover 18 months of service history. Note also that the record low service problem levels shown on these charts were dramatically improved in the months following the intervals shown. Allocation failures actually set a record of two percent and stayed there for months. Past due dollars remained at less than $2,000 for months, being as low as zero dollars regularly.

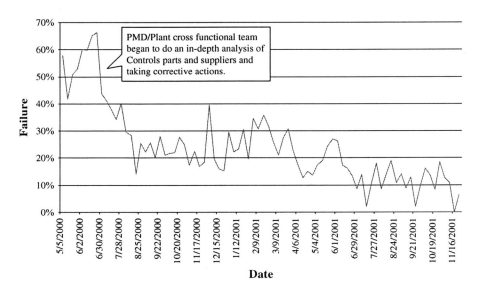

Figure 7A: Controls allocation failure history. Allocation failures are a measure of service problems where less is better. Allocation failures measure the percentage of incoming orders that do not have product in stock for immediate shipment. Service continued to improve in the months after this chart was developed for a total failure reduction of 95 percent.

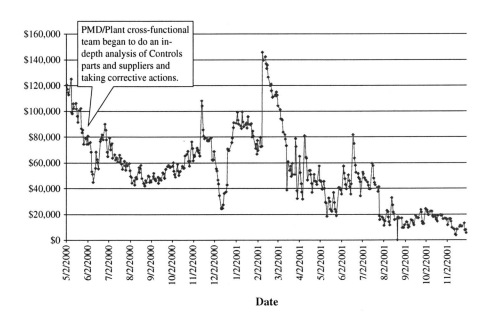

Figure 7B: Controls past due dollars. Past due dollars is another measure of service where less is better. Past due dollars measure the total value of late orders. Service continued to improve in the months after this chart was printed for a total 99 percent reduction in past due dollars.

HOW DOES THE PEOPLE CONNECTION WORK?

The Process gets the entire team to focus on the vision and the steps to get there, rather than on their current situation. The vision needs to be something the team can get excited about or else the problems will distract them. In reality, most of these problems really aren't that important, because some are perceptions and many others aren't worth the effort to solve them. These problems look significant and daunting when they are the team's focus.

I once had an assignment to work on a host of problems that was overwhelming our maintenance department. I believed strongly in involving the people doing the job, but I had not yet learned to value the vision. What I did, therefore, was involve all the maintenance guys in solving their own problems. That effort went just marvelously for months. The maintenance men were relieved and excited that their problems were finally being solved. But one day, as we approached the bottom of the list, progress slowed dramatically. I finally confronted the maintenance guys with this question: "You really don't want these problems solved, do you?" The lead man responded with, "No we don't. If we solve the rest of these problems then we won't have anything to bitch about." This is one more reason not to focus on the problems.

Arriving at a common vision requires a lot of time, effort, and reflection. Hashing through a vision statement in one or two long sessions is a waste of time, because it ignores the reflection time that is so important. A vision statement that cannot be instantly and enthusiastically recited from memory by each team member is also a waste. Five minutes of meeting time every week for two to three months is normally what is required to arrive at a powerful vision. The vision also requires many one-on-one discussions outside the meeting to ensure it is evolving properly.

Once the vision is in clear focus, there is a distinct improvement in how the team performs. Everyone notices the improvement because all of a sudden, things just click. All of a sudden, the team becomes much more efficient. Team members do not feel they are working any harder, yet the team is much more effective. This is called "synergy" and it occurs when almost all of the team members have internalized the same definition of the vision. A team should never expect more than 80 percent of the members to truly share the vision; but 80 percent is an overwhelming success.

It's important to understand the relationship between the focus of a team and its performance. *The more narrow the team focus, the greater the performance.* Figure 7C illustrates the following:

When people are brought together and given work to do, then they will be at the "culture" level of the pyramid on the left. Management can hire the best people with the best work ethics and the best values and will achieve team performance that is very good, but limited. There is only so much a well-meaning and hard-working group of people can accomplish without clear and commonly understood goals.

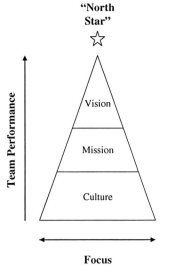

Figure 7C: Team Performance Pyramid

As an analogy, let's consider a sailing ship captain who hires the best riggers and the best sail trimmers. He has the best crew, and as they conscientiously go about their work, one crew member sets one sail in one direction, another sets another sail in a different direction, and so on, so that the boat's ability to achieve top speed is compromised. Every sail was rigged and trimmed just right, but they weren't set in the same direction.

The next level up, "mission", leads to improved team performance. This one gets everyone focused on the same goal. Following our analogy, the captain shouts out the direction they need to head in (the mission) and the crew springs into action to rig and trim the sails for that specific direction. The ship can now sail at top speed. Team performance has improved markedly. However, who knows where this course is going to take them? We can assume the captain knows – but shouldn't the crew know also?

The crew needs to know where the ship is going if the captain expects top performance. What the captain is ultimately aiming for is called "vision". If every crew member knew the vision was to set a sailing speed record between Bermuda and the French Riviera, what difference would it make in crew performance? The captain can't think of every little trick and remove every little obstacle to setting this record. The crew sees which lines (ropes) or sails need repaired or replaced before the captain does. Each crew member will be far more excited about setting a speed record than simply sailing in a direction that the captain dictates. This excitement will cause them to pay closer attention to the little things that will collectively make the big difference.

The vision is simple, clear and specific. Team performance is optimal when visions are precise. The mission is simply the way to get to that vision, and therefore can change from time to time as the need arises. The vision needs to be a pinpoint of light that never changes, like the North Star. For example, many people don't know that a sailing ship can actually sail against the wind by using a method called tacking. Tacking is directing the boat at a small angle away from the headwind and using the angle of the sails to drive the boat forward with enough power that it can overcome the headwind. Once the ship sails one tack for a time, then the ship is turned across the headwind so it now strikes the ship from the opposite side. Tacking then becomes a zig-zag path that keeps the ship moving against the wind. Tacking is the mission, or the way to get to the vision. The vision never changes, but the mission frequently does. The North Star is the pinpoint guiding light that the vision must be. Before the time of GPS (Global Positioning Systems) which identifies your exact location, all sailors navigated successfully by using the never-changing North Star — it was foolish to follow any other star because they always change positions in the night sky, which would lead to lost sailors and shipwrecks.

The challenge for the team leader is to ensure the proper environment has been created for this fragile vision development process. *The team leader needs <u>first</u> to believe that his or her team will be great. This is a process that cannot be seen to be believed, it must be believed first to be seen.* Why? *<u>The team can read a leader's mind.</u>* Team leaders need to stop looking at the faulty individuals on the team, and begin focusing on the team as a whole. Team leaders need to make it very safe for team members to express themselves openly and honestly. This allows the discrepancies in vision perceptions to be exposed and resolved. Exactly what the vision means needs to be internalized in the heart and mind of each of the team members.

To clarify and achieve the vision, the team leader needs to conduct a one-hour all-staff meeting once per week. The first five minutes of this meeting should be spent on the vision, the next 50 on what it will take to get there, and the last five minutes on plus/deltas. "Plus/deltas" is short for "What are we doing well and what can we do better?" The five-minute time slot for the vision should be a standing agenda topic for at least two to three months. This meeting needs to be the most important one on the leader's agenda and no other activities should interfere with it.

The People Connection is a process that cannot be seen to be believed, it must be believed first to be seen.

This meeting needs to be consistent in its format, in its reports, and in the performance charts that hang on the wall. The paradox is that the

People Connection Process builds a team that is designed for maximum flexibility, responsiveness, and competence, yet it relies on simple things that are solid and fixed. It needs a stable foundation in order to respond quickly and precisely to the wind regardless of its fickleness and severity. One of Dr. Deming's 14 points[7] is "constancy of purpose". Dr. Deming was the architect of Japan's dramatic economic recovery, and his 14 points are a treasure trove of wisdom useful for today's enterprises. I believe he meant for us to stick to one vision. I believe he also meant for us to stick to values, meeting formats and traditions. All of these things will work together to provide the team with the stable foundation they need.

Individuals can process only so much change before they become overloaded and ineffective. The team, having a personality of its own, is more easily overwhelmed than most individuals. Though teams can be extremely effective, they require very sensitive and understanding leadership. One way to think that helps me is "don't make any sudden moves around your team". It's like a wild and powerful tiger that trainers need to respect – move too quickly and unexpectedly and somebody gets hurt. Treat it right, and its awesome power will be impressively displayed.

∞CHAPTER 8: MAXIMIZING YOUR INFLUENCE

WINNING THE "HEART AND SOUL" OF THE TEAM

Our team made a significant discovery when we were conducting SPI (Statistical Process Improvement) training for the Foams Plant. Though we didn't realize it at first, we were definitely connecting with the team's heart and soul. The most remarkable example of this was the maintenance group.

The maintenance group had long been recognized as an underperforming bunch of prima donnas who just needed to be replaced. Our goal as trainers, of course, was to teach SPI, with a very heavy emphasis on teamwork. One maintenance person, Larry James, was one of the most notorious. He had one foot on a slippery banana peel and the other outside the gate, which meant his manager was looking for a way to fire him. We were amazed when Larry began responding positively and enthusiastically to our training.

Larry publicly applauded our teamwork lessons during training and declared that he thought they would work. He sounded so sincere that I made a prediction to my boss. I predicted this training would actually change the attitudes of many of our team members, and that some of our worst employees would become some of our best. Months later, we found that prediction to be true. Larry quickly advanced to an informal position of positive and visible leadership. He actually led an effort to improve one of our processes which involved a capital expenditure of $260,000. Larry was right. The People Connection did work.

A fascinating incident occurred before Larry actually got this far. A few months after the original SPI training, a team of machine operators, maintenance people, and supervisors were trying to decide how we were going to ensure that machine change-overs were executed correctly. One of the machine operators said he didn't believe other operators would follow through unless they had a supervisor to follow up on them. Larry's response was immediate and emphatic. He said, "If someone had held a gun to my head before SPI training and told me to say that people would actually be committed to their work and complete it faithfully, then they would've had to shoot me. What I have seen since the training is a conscientiousness that I would never have thought possible. There's no doubt in my mind that if the operators understand what needs to be done they will do it!" Larry *bought into what we were teaching, and was selling it to others!*

There was also an abundance of other evidence that we were winning over the Foams Plant. Remember the letter from Frank (chapter 2) that said we were an 11 on a scale of one to 10? He spent most of his time with our team members *without* the supervisors. Why? Frank knew that *cultural change happens in the heart and soul of the team, not in the reports of managers and supervisors or in the processes and programs that are imposed upon the team.* It was obvious to Frank that we had made the change.

You may recall what we heard from the Consultant and Corporate Quality Assurance when they conducted an audit of the Foams Plant SPI program. Our program was further along *after one year* than any other program they had ever seen. Keith Baker, our plant manager, said, "Through interviews and completed questionnaires from associates [team members]they also found that our knowledge and use of SPI and Juran principles [Dr. Juran was the problem-solving contemporary of Dr. Deming] were significantly higher than plant norms. Lastly, the understanding on the part of all associates that (company) management is committed to the program of constant quality improvement was understood and accepted by 87 percent of the individuals polled. This is the highest acceptance number our auditors have ever seen!"

Cultural change happens in the heart and soul of the team, not in the reports of managers and supervisors or in the processes and programs that are imposed upon the team.

The audit team also mentioned that the Foams Plant's progress in the first year was greater than one of the Big Three automaker's first ten years, and it employed one of the world's best consultants during that time. However, it isn't fair to blame the consultant, because he was aware of what was wrong and "fired" this automaker three times. This progress demonstrates that *heart and soul trumps talent*.

What captured the interest, commitment and enthusiasm of our associates, both hourly and salaried? I believe they saw their chance to be great and to be a part of something great, and this is what excited them. Profits soared. Supervisors reported that people were now solving their own problems. Team members would come in from vacation for team meetings rather than miss them.

A group of hourly paid team members volunteered to address the Foams Plant attendance policy. Management was fed up with all the complaints about the policy's strictness and welcomed the assistance from this team. However, everyone was stunned with the group's recommendation. They recommended that the days of absence allowed before termination be *significantly reduced*. This made it clear that team members want their team mates to shoulder their share of the workload. Management was amazed by how the workforce so thoroughly and completely bought into the People Connection.

> *Heart and soul trumps talent.*

INFLUENCE ALL DECISIONS

A lot of enthusiasm and activity can create chaos and headaches if leaders aren't prepared. *Establishing a clear, universally held vision is critical to controlling all of the energy generated by the People Connection.* A healthy team or organization requires a tremendous number of decisions to keep it going. The old style of controlling decisions, commonly called "micromanagement", is an *ineffective* way to control a team. Team members are fully aware that micromanagement severely throttles a team's performance, but they usually don't say anything because they don't want to upset the boss. Don't mistake their desire to make their own decisions as self-centered, short-sighted, arrogant, or disrespectful. Allowing them to make their own decisions is ultimately more effective and efficient, as it significantly grows and strengthens the team.

A Chinese proverb goes: "Give a man a fish and he will eat for a day. Teach him how to fish and he will eat for a lifetime." Let your team "fish" and they will grow and thrive. That is how they were designed. If the team is "given fish" because someone else can provide "better fish", then the team will remain stunted and dependent.

Micromanagement seriously inhibits the performance of a team. It also sends a number of inappropriate and negative messages:

∞   Team members cannot be trusted to make their own decisions.
∞   The boss is the only one capable of making the right decisions.
∞   The team members' time is not as important as the boss's because they're always waiting on the boss for the answer.
∞   Decision-making is a privilege of power which only the boss is entitled to.
∞

All of these messages hurt the team's morale and performance. The biggest damage is to the decision-making dynamic among team members. Every day, hundreds – perhaps thousands – of decisions need to get made quickly and effectively. Ideally, they need to get made with all of the right information and a full understanding of the issues and consequences. Expecting the boss, or a delegate, to make all these decisions is unrealistic. Decisions that can be made by the team should be; decisions that need to be made by the leader jointly with the team should be; and those that can only be made by the leader should be made by the leader.

> *Establishing a clear, universally held vision is critical to controlling all of the energy generated by the People Connection.*

Leaders need to accept that not all team decisions will _appear_ to be best decisions. Obviously, the team will make some bad ones, but unless they are going to hurt someone or break a law, then they should be allowed to carry them out and learn from their mistakes. Mistakes are some of the best training ever, so their costs are usually well worth it. Leaders also need to accept that most of these decisions are being made with knowledge and understanding they don't have. This fact will naturally lead to discrepancies between what the leader feels are good decisions and what the team feels are good decisions. More often than not, team decisions that look bad initially, turn out to be great decisions in hindsight.

I once mentored a team that I regrettably neglected for what seemed like more important priorities at the time. This team was a group of machine operators responsible for raising the efficiencies of their equipment. Five times they asked me if I saw any problems with ideas they wanted to implement, and five times I saw no problem – nor potential – but I didn't discourage them. After about three months of this, my boss asked me how my team was able to achieve efficiency gains of 15 percent in just three months when four percent *per year* was the norm. I was stunned and embarrassed because I had no clue. I quickly investigated and discovered their ho-hum suggestions had in fact raised efficiencies at a rate *15 times the average annual rate. Leaders should never impose their standards for good ideas on their group.* Results are what counts and the team usually knows best how to get them.

The best way for a leader to influence all decisions is to ensure that the team has a firm grasp of the vision, and let them make the decisions on how to get there. Timely and informed decisions are essential for any organization, and these are best made by the team. *Let the vision – not the leader – influence the team's decisions.*

DRIVE WASTE OUT OF ALL PROCESSES

A tremendous amount of waste exists in every organization, due mainly to an imperfect understanding of the goal. Each team member naturally has difficulties in determining exactly what and how much they have to do in order to achieve the team's objectives. *As a result, their tasks are overdone, underdone, or done late.*

It's a waste to overdo tasks, because the extra effort isn't necessary. For example, one person may feel a job is not done until the envelope is sealed. The next person down the line now needs to steam open the envelope to do their job. Sealing it was overdoing the job and led to the wasted efforts of sealing and steaming open the envelope.

Under doing the job is also a waste. For example, the first envelope stuffer may have left out a document, so the second one has to get up from the work station and go pick up the missing document from the first stuffer. Either the first stuffer didn't understand the goal or simply failed to perform, both of which led to rework which usually involves both wasted efforts and materials.

It's also a waste to do a job late because it creates idle time for others as they wait on the late job to be completed. If the first stuffer were working toward a 10 a.m. deadline, and the second stuffer were ready at 9 a.m., then the second stuffer could waste as much as an hour in waiting on the first one.

The legitimacy and power of the team's vision make it much easier for people to challenge and hold each other accountable for finding and eliminating such wastes. Teams also need to feel compelled to eliminate wastes caused by doing things the way they've always been done. Time and circumstances are constantly changing which means we must continuously search for waste. The People Connection is an effective and efficient mechanism for driving the improvement activities necessary to reduce these wastes.

Lean is one of today's best-known ways of reducing waste. It has proven itself effective by focusing on one-piece flows and using specialized tools such as value-stream mapping (analytical tool for streamlining processes) and identifying value-added and non-value added activities. Many non-value added activities are then removed because customers aren't willing to pay for them. Single-piece flow is simply passing one product at a time to the next person to do their part instead of waiting for the entire batch to be complete. This reduces the amount of work in process and the waste that comes from an entire batch being bad. Value stream mapping is very useful for understanding what the process is and how it can be improved. Lean reaches its maximum potential when used by teams who are already proficient in reducing wastes mentioned previously.

DRIVE VARIATION OUT OF ALL PROCESSES

Variation is another form of waste. Variation creates rejects, which usually require extra time and materials to rework or replace. Variation is inherent in all processes, but is particularly wasteful in processes that are not well-defined or well-controlled. This lack of definition and control means the work is being done differently – no matter how slightly – each time. These wastes can be as simple as having to slow down and think about how the work needs to be done.

This point came home loud and clear when assemblers in the West Coast Plant fell 30 percent short of the Decatur Plant's production rates. Six other plants, which included three outside the company, were struggling just like we were. We finally discovered that Decatur's secret was to remove process variation.

Variation is regularly being addressed by a popular process called "Six Sigma". This is a sophisticated process using powerful statistical tools and an infrastructure of talent and expertise, with martial arts titles like "Black Belts" and "Green Belts". The titles reflect the high degree of discipline and commitment that are required to make these tools work as designed.

Six Sigma tools are powerful in solving problems in almost any kind of organization or team.

However, Six Sigma requires a significant amount of time and resources to address one problem at a time. This disadvantage makes it impractical for solving every problem in an organization. Six Sigma should be reserved for only the more difficult and complex problems. Easier problems should be solved by one or two people employing a much less formal process.

Asking team members to identify and eliminate causes of process variation will result in real improvements. One way of doing this is to ask a series of "Why?" questions. For example, a company is supposed to deliver product to a customer on time every time. However, product delivery times are unpredictable and often late so the customers get upset. So we ask the team why it's late, and we hear it's because the warehouse received it late. We then ask "Why?" again and find out that manufacturing was late in shipping it. A few more "why?" questions and we finally arrive at the *root cause,* which is that manufacturing purchase orders are only issued on Mondays. The team discovers a solution that allows orders to be placed daily so that production will have parts when they need them. Whether Six Sigma is utilized formally, or informally as in this example, it's an important contributor to improving team performance.

The best way for a leader to influence all decisions is to ensure that the team has a firm grasp of the vision.

∞ CHAPTER 9: AIM HIGH AND HIT THE TARGET!

DRIVE FOR A COMMON UNDERSTANDING OF THE GOAL – TWO TEAM STORIES

Bobby Jones, a team leader in the Polyethylene Plant, approached me one day and reported he was having serious difficulties getting his team to perform. All the members wanted to do, he said, was argue in the team meetings. Regular attendance and follow-through on assignments was also a problem. I asked Bobby if all his team members understood the goal and he said they did. They had carefully constructed a mission statement when the team first began. They had followed the traditional process of laboring over every word, finally gave up, and assigned some startled victim to finish it outside the meeting. They had all approved the mission statement but found they could not accomplish it.

I then asked Bobby if I might attend his next team meeting to discuss the team's vision. We discovered they all had distinctly different ideas about their goal *even though it read the same for each of them*. There are almost always many misunderstandings and disagreements in mission statements, goals, and visions. I made the point earlier about stopping a team in the midst of conflict and asking the basic questions about the vision and how to get there. That's what we did in this meeting and quickly arrived at a consensus. Bobby had no more problems with his team from that point on, and they went on to accomplish their mission in an exemplary fashion.

Another example of a misunderstanding of the goal occurred in the Reclaim Room of the Polyethylene Plant. The production of plastic bags and stretch wrap creates a lot of scrap that, for ecological and economic reasons, needs to be recycled. This scrap film is ground into small pieces, like confetti. These small pieces are sent to an extruder, which is a machine that melts down the confetti and extrudes it into condensed pellets similar to popcorn kernels. These pellets are now in the form that can best be used by the equipment that makes the finished goods, which are stretch film and plastic bags.

The Reclaim Room was having problems working together and everyone could see it. When I talked with the supervisor about an idea to correct this situation, he stressed how often he and others had tried to correct the problem without success. He held no hope for my idea, although he welcomed my efforts.

The Reclaim Room was a 24/7, or around-the-clock, seven-day-a-week operation. It was staffed by a number of shift crews. The problem was that one of the crews would always run the easy to recycle material and leave the hard to recycle material for the other shifts. The result was inconsistencies in shift performance and in regrind quality. These inconsistencies, or *variations*, created waste because of the constant adjustments that both regrind operators and finished goods operators needed to make. Regrind operators were rewarded individually, so it was natural they'd run the easy stuff whenever they had the chance.

To complicate matters, there was one particular reclaim operator, Macumbe Boudreau, who was being blamed for all the problems by his fellow operators. He was the one who had by far the best shift performance and really was running most of the easy-to-run material. He was sneaky enough, however, that his supervisor couldn't catch him. Macumbe was from deep within the Louisiana bayous and looked the part of the swamp rat — short, skinny, shifty-eyed, and more than a bit spooky. All the other operators were convinced he was into voodoo and was sprinkling pixie dust on their scrap film so they would run into production problems. The curse of the voodoo hung heavy over the reclaim department.

Rather than trying to trap Macumbe, my approach was to change all the operators' vision and thinking. We didn't change the way they got rewarded, because we realized that wouldn't fix the problem. Even if they were rewarded as a team, Macumbe and others like him would still run the easy stuff if they could. I spent a few weeks, just a few minutes at a time, with these operators developing a team vision. They began to understand the value of consistent shift performances and consistent regrind material. I spent time helping them to understand that their individual performance measures would improve <u>only if they worked to ensure that the performance of the entire team improved.</u> I met a lot of resistance at first, because they were convinced that the only way to the best collective performance was through the best individual performance. This is a classic misunderstanding of many leaders, too. I was finally able to get them to accept that maybe there was a better way, and they were ready to give it a try.

Within 30 days, they improved their total regrind efficiencies by 15 percent and, of course, their individual shift performances shot up as well. That convinced them. *They now went out of their way to help one another!* Macumbe was even praised by his fellow operators because he was so helpful. Complaints about the other shifts, which are very common in shift operations, evaporated. And furthermore, they were enthusiastic about what they had learned.

These experiences – and many more like them – have made it clear to me that almost every facility and every team have goal misconnects similar to these. Whenever this happens, always stop the work and ask the question: what are we trying to accomplish? It usually takes only a short discussion to get the team back on track. Focusing on vision almost always puts the immediate obstacles in perspective, which usually means they are either cast aside as irrelevant, or overcome quickly in the rush to the goal.

A shared vision is critical for teamwork, but what if disagreement arises over *how* to get there? A little exploration into the merits of the different paths to the goal will help reduce the intensity of the disagreement – usually. If that doesn't work, then it helps to point out *there is oftentimes more than one right answer.* A tremendous amount of time can be wasted arguing about which answer is best, as if there is only one that is superior. That may be true, but the best answer is almost always the one that the team really *wants* to own. Inferior solutions implemented by committed and determined teams deliver better results than superior solutions implemented by teams who don't believe in them. If the team chooses the solution they *prefer* from among all those they are debating, they will be better off.

PRESS THEM TO TAKE ACTION

Action is effective at getting people to fully commit to the vision. Action creates the opportunity for people to invest themselves. Once invested, they want that investment to pay off. Action provides valuable experience and insight that will increase their confidence and the quality of their decisions. Action increases engagement, because most people can relate better to actions than they can to ideas. Mental visualization is not as common as most leaders assume. When people have the live action visuals recorded in their minds, it's much easier for them to engage in the team meetings, which is where most commitment begins.

An old exhortation says, "Do something even if it's wrong." A lot of wisdom resides in that command, although carried to its extreme the saying leads to the reckless and wasteful "shoot from the hip" mentality. However, this command actually helps a team who needs the learning experiences that are necessary for making better decisions faster. As in so many things, there are trade-offs. Careful and deliberate decision-making needs to be carefully balanced, or traded off against instinctive decision-making depending on the seriousness of the decisions. Most decisions are best made quickly and therefore, preferably, by instinct. Instinctive decision-making needs to be encouraged and practiced to be perfected. The People Connection is designed to balance deliberation and instinct as well as produce an abundance of decisions that receive quick feedback.

Team confidence will then quickly grow from the inevitable learning and successes that result.

Action to increase buy-in and resolve are important, but action that moves the team closer to the goal is what we want most of all. How do we get more of what we want? The answer, of course, is to keep the vision in focus and to keep the team working on the actions to achieve it. The team has a tremendous reservoir of ideas that can be tried, but there are limits. Their paradigms may blind them to some ideas that they should be trying, so including "outsiders" in brainstorming will help uncover those hidden ideas. Outsiders include those who are familiar to the group but not experts – someone from a different team or department, for example. Outsiders may also include suppliers or customers who know something about the product or service. Trying any and all ideas that are aimed at the vision will eventually lead to success.

Decisions should not be re-analyzed outside the meeting because the team has already deliberated on them. Just implement them. One of the most common pet peeves is an organization's inability to make and implement decisions. Bureaucracy is famous for that. Bureaucracy, which is necessary to coordinate and control an organization, can obviously choke it, as well as give the cartoonists more than enough material to keep us all entertained. There is a time for everything...a time for planning, and a time for action and these times need to be kept separated. Sometimes it's appropriate to respond to Monday morning quarterbacks with, "I'm sorry, but the ship has already sailed. The decision has been made and will be implemented." Timely action is necessary for an organization's success, so the bureaucracy needs to be adjusted to accommodate that need.

This push for action may bewilder some team members at first, because they are not used to it; but it will become enthusiastically accepted as the team gains experience with it. Enthusiasm builds as they attempt, fail, try again, and ultimately succeed. As this enthusiasm builds, the quality of their decisions improves, and their work begins to impress all observers.

Many believe the only way to create a high-performing team is to replace existing team members with better performers. The People Connection disproves this belief. The normal team selection processes are usually effective, so the team make-up is almost never an issue. It's the emphasis on personal involvement in the action that makes a strong team.

WHAT ARE WE DOING WELL, AND WHAT CAN WE DO BETTER?

I believe human beings are wired for change. Unfortunately, this wiring is often short-circuited because change is usually associated with loss – probably because of bad experiences with change processes. How often have we grown tired of something and wanted a change? As we reflect on our lives, we can see that we have gone through many changes, and these changes, by and large, have been beneficial. I believe the key is to use a change process that is in harmony with the wiring that our team already has. The People Connection is that process.

Six Sigma has popularized the term "plus/deltas", which is the clever little title for meeting critiques. If the critique is a positive ("attaboy" or "attagirl"), it is called a "plus" which, of course, everybody likes to get. If the critique is for something that should be changed, then it is labeled a "delta". Delta is the Greek symbol that means change. No one conducting training, meetings, or giving a report wants a delta. Deltas are seen as negative in our society, although Six Sigma experts stress that they are simply opportunities for improvement, which should be appreciated and not avoided. These experts actually call them "gifts" to make them more palatable. Knowing that pain and disappointment are often hidden behind the smile that accepts these deltas and this line from the experts, I believe it's better to be realistic than idealistic.

Though it's a very subtle change in semantics, I've found that the question "what are we doing well, and what can we do better?" works better than the term plus/deltas. The implication in this question is that what's being done now is okay because it just is; but since we're committed to improvement, let's think of something we can do better. This is better because it focuses on improvement opportunities, which we really must find, and takes our focus away from what is "wrong". The word "wrong (or delta)" is like the word "problem". The People Connection carefully avoids both and relies on the vision to drive progress, not problems or deltas.

Everything we do from team meetings to how the team is working together outside the meetings should be subjected to continuous improvement. Constant improvement needs to be a welcome and rewarding drive within each team member. This drive takes time to develop. Thousands of small changes and small improvements are the only way to lasting and significant increases both in individual and team performance. *__What we are doing well celebrates our progress. What we can do better gives us hope for the future.__*

∞CHAPTER 10: HOW TO SUPPORT THE PEOPLE CONNECTION

CONSTANTLY MONITOR AND MAINTAIN THE PROCESS

–

THE WEST COAST PLANT STORY

My next job after the Conyers Plant was as Engineering Manager with the West Coast Plant. This plant, too, was struggling. Though I was confident, the situation was actually worse than I thought. Productivity wasn't meeting expectations; component inventory accuracy was unacceptable; morale was low. And things were growing steadily worse. The new plant manager turned up the heat, but it failed to stem the tide of declining productivity.

One of the key problems was inventory accuracy, and the material handlers were blamed for it. Material handler re-training was suggested as a remedy and promptly completed. However, the decline continued and the staff's anxiety increased. Although my job description included neither material handlers nor training, I suggested that if the training were redesigned and redelivered, it would work. No one agreed at first – my proposal sounded too unconventional, too soft, and too far outside my "territory". However, the plant manager eventually, out of desperation, agreed and gave me 24 hours to organize the training and a week to get all the material handlers trained. This was generosity at its best, and at first glance looked every bit like one of those open mouth, insert foot situations. The material handling supervisor and I joined forces immediately and set a new goal: we would create an accurate inventory out of the mess we had. It didn't make sense to stop production and take a formal inventory because of the time and expense required, as well as the fact that it would not stay accurate given the problems we had.

We asked ourselves what it would take to <u>*create*</u> an accurate inventory on the fly and <u>***not***</u> what it would take to solve our problems. Within 24 hours we had what we thought were the answers and our training program. We started delivering the training in earnest the very next day. It was unusual training because it was more structured dialogue than training. We shared with the material handlers what the goal was, why we needed it, some suggestions for improvement, and then supported the implementation of their ideas. Inventory accuracy at that time was less than 70 percent and was declining rapidly. Anything less than 95% means trouble. It began improving as soon as we began the training and got to the mid-90's in about a month.

Every material handler was focused on the goal. We didn't waste time identifying what was wrong, placing blame, or fixing what was broken. This approach also helped quietly eliminate some of the causal factors that material handlers took it upon themselves to correct as they took ownership of inventory accuracy.

Though recovery was beginning, the long-running plant melt-down had already created irreparable damage to our plant manager's career with the company. He was fired and I was named as his replacement. I received about as many condolences as congratulations. One guy actually said I must have been the last man standing, which made me realize that the rest of the staff had apparently run and hid from the assignment.

I received about as many condolences as congratulations. One guy actually said I must have been the last man standing, which made me realize that the rest of the staff had apparently run and hid from the assignment.

We applied the same process to the plant that we used for improving inventory accuracy. We improved efficiencies approximately 20 percent within the first couple of months. Morale was way up. We were looking good, except for one thing. A couple of hourly associates and a supervisor began giving me reports of mistreatment by one of the managers. I had been uneasy about this manager even before these reports, but had nothing specific to go on. One of my staff members shared this same concern. I felt this problem needed attention in spite of limited information and the fact that this manager had received many excellent performance appraisals.

Meanwhile, we also had to improve our materials flow as well as inventory accuracy. This meant significantly changing the layout of the facility without allowing production to slip. We met the challenge through creative planning and execution, succeeding well ahead of expectations, and with no disruption of production. This was a real tribute to the robustness of the organization we had just revitalized – *with the same people*.

We also had a labor contract renewal coming up. Finances were tight, so we couldn't be liberal in our wage commitments. Even so, we stretched the best we could and came up with the best contract we had in years. In a stroke of poor timing, there was a burst of publicity about our company's billion dollar sales milestone. The union membership was now starting to factor those billion dollars into what they thought they should get in the new contract. Unfortunately, little thought was given to how much it *cost* to generate that sales number.

As contract negotiation time approached, the drama with our problem manager also intensified. My boss stiffly challenged my assertions about this manager, but we finally reached full agreement. I had to place this manager on 90-day objectives (basically probation), because this was company policy and the right thing to do. Tensions and anxieties increased as the deadline approached and it became more apparent the manager was not going to make it.

I also got a number of calls and visits from corporate Human Resources challenging my position with this manager. I stood by my assessment, even though much of it rested on the observations of other people.

As if a plant turn-around, contract negotiations, and a problem manager weren't challenges enough, we were also falling short in our ability to assemble emergency light fixtures for our Decatur Plant. We were not able to achieve any better than 70 percent of Decatur's production rates. Every other plant, six in all, could do no better than we could. We then assigned our best assemblers to the job to no avail. We asked for assistance from Decatur and an expert came to help us. We also sent people to Decatur to see if they could figure out how Decatur was doing it. All of this accomplished nothing. I then requested a video be made of the Decatur assembly operations, so we could study them more closely.

When the tape arrived, we spent hours examining it. No one could see what Decatur was doing differently, and they certainly didn't seem to be working any harder or faster. After countless viewing sessions, I finally saw that the Decatur assemblers never varied their routine in the slightest from fixture to fixture. Every move they made was identical to the fixture before; they were performing just like machines. By contrast, our assemblers always mixed up their routine to reduce monotony. I requested that the assembly manager instruct our assemblers to copy the Decatur assemblers. The manager agreed but couldn't get them to comply.

I then requested that temporary employees be hired right off the street with no previous assembly experience. These temps were instructed to follow the Decatur method exactly. Within one week, these temps were matching Decatur's rates! We had just stumbled on "standard work", which is a Lean term for doing a series of tasks exactly the same way and in the same order each time. We didn't know that Decatur had implemented Lean several years earlier. The Decatur "expert" apparently had forgotten, even though the assemblers didn't.

Contract negotiations were stalled because the union leadership felt they needed a bigger cut of the billion-dollars. I countered with a quick course in business economics, and they finally understood and agreed to our contract proposal. Many of us were now concerned about whether the leadership could convince the membership. Strong radical elements among the membership had a lot of influence, and would be difficult to convince. Each employee had a company coffee cup proclaiming the billion dollar milestone. I wanted to get rid of mine – it was giving me a headache.

> **Lean's standard work can increase productivity by 30 percent.**

The proposed contract was presented to the membership, and much to our shock and dismay they voted to strike on the first vote. The first vote is usually a simple rejection, which returns both parties to the bargaining table; it's never a strike. To make things worse, we had frequently made it clear that we had no financial wiggle-room for a strike. I guessed no one believed us.

When I asked the union leadership for the reason, they said they "*honestly didn't know and were just as puzzled as we were.*" The best they could come up with was "*maybe* there was some bad blood between management and the membership." My only consolation, though not really comforting, was they weren't upset at me, personally. Now what?

It seemed like everyone showed up for picket duty the next couple of weeks, which is also highly unusual. I asked a number of them why they were striking and all they knew is that they were told to be there! What made it even stranger was there were no picket signs. We were quickly shipping out tooling and other production capabilities to other plants because of intense pressure to maintain service. We were rapidly approaching the point of no return, and still no one would talk. The shutdown I wanted to avoid was becoming a reality.

The time quickly arrived for what is called "decision-bargaining", where the union and management have one last chance to re-negotiate the conditions of keeping the plant open. It was at this decision-bargaining session that we finally discovered the reason for the strike. *The report of bad blood between management and the union membership was centered on one particular manager. This was the same manager I was in the process of terminating. If I had not listened to a couple of hourly associates and one new supervisor, I would not have gotten as close as I did to terminating this manager in time.* If the termination would have been just a week or so earlier, there may not have been a strike. So close, but yet so far away!

There were two important lessons in this experience:

1. *Oftentimes, it's only the plant manager or leader who understands how fast the clock is ticking. Both the leader and the team need to remember that.* Leaders will have a tendency to be impatient and to want quick results. Teams will have a tendency to take all the time necessary to do the job right. The leader and the team need to work closely together to keep these two tendencies in the proper balance.

2. *It's necessary to trust others to help fill in the blind spots that all leaders have.*

In the final analysis, the West Coast Plant responded very favorably to the People Connection, up until the radical elements surfaced during the strike. Some of the more radical and influential of these elements were actually in another part of the business (covered by the same contract) over which the plant had no influence. In spite of losing the plant to an unfortunate strike, the plant improved efficiencies by 20 percent in just a couple of months. Inventory accuracy was corrected in just one month. Morale was skyrocketing even though time had run out on a resentment that came so close to resolution. Once again, a trying situation further refined the People Connection.

> *Oftentimes, only the plant manager or leader understands how fast the clock is ticking. Both the leader and the team need to remember that.*

Leaders won't always get a clear picture of what is going on from the weekly team meeting. They need to regularly stop and talk with people at their work stations to ask how things are going for them. The leader should also ask, at the appropriate time, how well everything is working for the team. Depending on the current working environment, the answers from everyone may be honest and straightforward, or there may be just a few who are brave enough to answer honestly. If only a few raise issues and the rest are positive, then give those issues careful consideration before responding to them. It's crucial these comments be accepted graciously and thoughtfully, because they may be the tip of an iceberg.

Take the time to carefully consider these comments in the context of how the team is working together. Addressing these concerns too quickly can lead to problems. Sudden moves will almost always be regretted, or worse, cause invisible damage. Team members who bring up sensitive issues need to trust they won't lead to an over-reaction. Of course, some of the stuff we hear will be false or twisted, but a sincere interest in their thoughts and feelings is not often abused. Time will help sort out the twisted stuff.

TRACK AND DISPLAY THE TEAM'S PROGRESS TOWARD THE GOAL

One often-quoted adage says, "What gets measured gets improved." This is true. If a team takes the time and effort to measure and talk about those measurements, then those things will improve with seemingly little effort. This happens because the attention given these measurements focuses the team.

Measurements directly related to the goal will get more interest, more support, and a higher level of engagement. Keeping the team engaged also requires regular feedback on how well they are doing in achieving the goal. Written feedback that is convenient to the team at all times is the best way to do this.

If you recall from the axe experiment in chapter two, people need to see the chips fly. Chopping with a dull axe really isn't any harder than chopping with a sharp one if the chips didn't matter. However, they do matter as the experiment showed. Remember that *nobody* could finish the hour chopping with a dull axe. A person's need to be great drives their need to see the results of **their** efforts, and when they can't, their performance declines. Or worse yet, as in the case of the dull axe, they quit. They can quit by walking out the door, or worse yet, quit secretly at their work stations.

Highly visible measurements need to be posted on the meeting room wall and ideally at the team's work stations. These measurements will serve the following purposes:

∞ Visibility – shows how well the team is making the chips fly.

∞ Focus - it emphasizes the importance of the measurement.

∞ Multiply results - it will positively influence the innumerable and invisible decisions individual team members make outside the meetings.

∞ Engage – discussing these measurements and creating action items to improve them will increase the team's ownership and commitment to the goal.

The best way to show progress is a chart such as the ones shown in Figures 7A and 7B on page 61. These charts show the value of the measurement over time, which is important because continuous improvement takes time. The dates are in sequence on the horizontal axis and the measurement value is on the vertical axis. Making notes on the chart about key events as shown in 7A and 7B also provide valuable feedback.

Measurement techniques and chart formats can become far more sophisticated with various kinds of control charts and trend analyses. Many excellent resources are available that detail these, so there's no reason to address them here. It should be remembered, though, that these more advanced tools can make the team more effective in the *technical* aspect of their work. However, the basic chart shown in this book is all that is necessary to completely engage a team.

KEEP A RECORD OF YOUR MEETINGS AND OBSERVATIONS

If you have ever driven west towards Pike's Peak in Colorado you probably noticed it can be seen from about 125 miles away, although it seems like only four or five. It seems so close when it suddenly appears above the horizon. But impatience quickly sets in when it seems to be taking forever to get there. However, the rearview mirror reveals the road behind disappearing at expressway speeds. You really are making good time but it sure doesn't look like it as you are staring at the mountain. The People Connection invariably suffers from the same phenomenon.

It's therefore important, for team leaders especially, to keep a written record of the team meetings and their observations. This written record, or "rearview mirror" will help the leader overcome impatience, frustration, and concern that the Process might not be working as it should. Every team I have worked with has appeared to move at a snail's pace; and every leader feels the same impatience, frustration, and concern. The leader's exasperation, unfortunately, can send the wrong message to the team, or cause the leader to make rash decisions which will hamper the team's progress. The written record will remind everyone how fast they really are moving.

A single page of weekly meeting minutes and observations on how the team is performing makes the best written record. More than a page becomes a burden. Anything less could leave out important information. The reflections should be jointly developed in a short post-meeting debrief between the leader and process partner(s). Process partners will be described at length in just a minute.

> *It's important to keep a written record of the team meetings and observations.*

These written records are also great for celebrations. The best celebrations are those that celebrate the journey, not just the destination. Ninety-five percent of a team's efforts are spent in working hard on the daily grind, and through setbacks, obstacles and frustrations. Only five percent can actually be called success, or arriving at the goal. Celebrations should celebrate the 95 percent as well as the 5 percent. Reliving the 95% is enjoyable and fulfilling for the entire team. (This idea originated from a book called Incredibly American: Releasing the Heart of Quality by Marilyn R. Zuckerman and Lewis J. Hatala.)

DEPEND ON A PROCESS PARTNER WHO CAN SEE OUR BLIND SPOTS

A process partner is one who can see what we can't, and one we can always count on to be truthful. The truth we need is more than just ethical truth; we need what is accurate and reliable. Honesty without accuracy is insufficient. Tact is a great plus, but it shouldn't take any edge off the truth.

A good process partner(s) completes a leader's field of vision. It is essential that a leader has a full and clear field of vision.

Everyone has blind spots – everyone! No one is a superman or super-woman. Unfortunately, almost everyone except for the leader is aware of that. We can't be fooled by the compliments, the displayed respect, and the affirming words. In the words of John Wooden, widely regarded as the greatest college coach in history with an unmatched record of 10 <u>NCAA</u> National Championships: "You can't let *praise* or criticism get to you. It is a weakness to get caught up in either one. Some criticism will be honest and some won't. Some praise you will deserve and some you won't. You have to take both in the same light." Ironically, we actually become more "super" if we become humble enough to follow that advice.

It takes courage to admit we don't know and can't see everything. In some environments this courage might feel impossible to summon…if we're in charge of a bunch of intransigent kids or working in a really bad political environment, for example. However, it's surprising how much more a team respects and appreciates leaders who are humble and coura-geous enough to admit that they can't see and know everything.

I began learning this lesson more than 20 years ago when I was new to training the Foams Plant employees on SPI (Statistical Process Improve-ment). This was a three-day training program that involved 20 to 22 em-ployees each. Those who trained me emphasized it was essential that I didn't make any mistakes in front of the group. To ensure that I wouldn't, I was supposed to call on someone from the group to work the problems on the flip charts in front of the class. I readily complied, since I was a new trainer and welcomed any opportunity to avoid embarrassing myself. This practice worked well until I ran into a group that wouldn't participate without dragging it out of them. We were falling behind as a result, so I started working the problems myself to catch up. And then that dreaded moment happened – I made a mistake in front of the class! I added a series of numbers incorrectly.

What happened next amazed me and forever convinced me that you must cheerfully place yourself at risk if you're going to lead others. When

I matter-of-factly admitted I made a mistake, and just as matter-of-factly corrected it, they opened up. Just as if I had flipped a switch, they were now participating. I had broken down a significant barrier to communication with this display of humility. I had no problems getting volunteers to work problems in front of this group or any other group from then on.

If we are real and honest with others, they will more than likely be real and honest with us. Some things they will try to tell us, however, we will not be able to see – as in never. Some things we can never see could be important enough to make a big difference to the team. So it's important that we find ways to fill these serious blind spots.

Certain people on our teams are quite perceptive about what is happening with the team. These are the people to listen to. If they are also well-respected and approachable by most, or all, of the team members, then we need to listen even more intensely. And, if we also have a solid trust relationship with these same people, then they could be our process partners.

ASSESS THE TEAM AFTER EVERY MEETING

Teams change very rapidly and rarely on a straight-line path. Watch closely or they will be zigging while we're zagging. Many significant changes in the team are subtle, and the leader must recognize them to provide the proper leadership. Leaders, therefore, need to carefully study the team's progress after each team meeting.

Watch who the team members are talking to. When they begin addressing one another, instead of just the team leader, they are making a breakthrough as a team. They are beginning to show that they feel empowered rather than directed. If normally quiet people begin participating, then we are connecting with people we really need to reach. This shows also that the leader is being successful in creating a safe environment for participation. The overall dynamics of the team meeting will tell a lot about how the team is doing outside the meeting as well. If they are working well together during the meeting, then chances are they are working well together outside the meeting.

Identifying and evaluating these clues is not a one-person job because they are too numerous and frequently too subtle for one person to catch. A half-hour or less debrief between leaders and their process partner(s) is essential. In this debrief, leaders should determine the adjustments they must make to their style – or agenda – for the next meeting. These adjustments will come surprisingly fast. These observations need to be recorded as mentioned earlier.

One word of caution about the debriefs: don't be discouraged if the team doesn't seem to be progressing as it should. Teams grow with a pace that is beset with many spurts and regressions. Growth spurts are encouraging, but they lull us into a sense of expectancy that all meetings should show progress. The regressions, therefore, are discouraging. If we look carefully at regressions, we will almost always find the seeds of further progress. A leader should always exhibit confidence that these seeds can be nourished into future success.

∞CHAPTER 11: JUMP-STARTING THE PEOPLE CONNECTION

"Leadership should be born out of the understanding of the needs of those who would be affected by it."
– Marian Anderson

Everything we have covered to this point shows how to support the team using the People Connection. We are now prepared for the most exciting step of all – turning it on. It's not any more difficult than hooking up a new computer or TV. Turning on a team requires looking the middle 60 percent straight in the eye, not showing any fear, and always doing the right things. Okay, getting two out of three is acceptable, since its okay to be scared. Doing the right things include:

1. Recognize who they are and what they need.
2. Disable the pecking order.
3. Get them to fit together as a team.
4. Regularly monitor that fit.

Establishing the vision and tracking progress are just as important, but they have been addressed earlier. Now we are going to get up close and personal.

THE 60 PERCENT ARE A GOLD MINE

The middle 60 percent outnumbers the other two groups combined by a factor of 50 percent. The 20 percent on the top are doing so much already; they really can't do much more. Though it shouldn't happen, they can be neglected and managed poorly and will probably continue to perform just fine. The 20 percent on the bottom can't or won't perform no matter how good the leadership is. A lot of time and effort can be invested in trying to train and motivate them, but this usually ends up in frustration and disappointment. The 60 percent in the middle are usually just idling along waiting for the right leadership to make them shine.

By no means should a team leader short-change the top and bottom 20 percents on training, attention, and leadership. Each team member and each group needs to be treated as much alike as possible. The three groups ideally require three distinctly different leadership styles, but only one style should be used. To use the People Connection effectively, *the leader's style should be geared for the 60 percent in the middle.*

We must remember that it's not always clear to a leader which group each team member belongs to. Leaders may "think" they know, but they are wrong much of the time. This uncertainty emphasizes the need to treat every team member with respect, and to treat them the same.

The team members, themselves, have a much better understanding of who is in each group. A team leader, as you might expect, should not consult individual team members about who is in which group. The words "snitch, rat, and back-stabbing" come to mind – if not your mind, then someone else's. It simply isn't worth the risk, so team leaders shouldn't do it.

To complicate matters even more, the groupings are not static, so team members will move from group to group with some regularity. A leader would be wise, therefore, to dismiss group membership information as impractical to obtain. In reality, the People Connection actually makes it unnecessary to know anyway. The team is oftentimes more effective than the leader in doing something about the 20 percent on the bottom, because of the unique advantages and leverage they have.

Leadership style should be geared for the 60 percent in the middle.

STOP THE CHICKENS BY DISABLING THE PECKING ORDER

To help engage the 60 percent, the leader should try to disable the "pecking order" tendency in the team. Pecking order is the natural tendency for individuals to demonstrate their superiority (or "significance") by showing dominance over others. That is one natural instinct we share with chickens. Some team members will shun, or treat disrespectfully, those they perceive are not supporting the team to their satisfaction...or those who appear to be of lesser social or professional status. The leader must ensure that this unhealthy practice is minimized, or it will inhibit the team's performance.

The best way to disable the "pecking order" is to take two to three minutes in each of a series of meetings to describe the following puzzle analogy until it is clear that the team understands it. Simply reminding them of it periodically for a few months or so after that is also necessary.

The analogy goes like this: Each person on the team is here for a reason and wouldn't be here if they weren't needed. *Each team member is a piece of the puzzle, and each one is needed to complete the picture.* It's impossible to perform as an excellent team without a complete picture. Never mind the details such as skills, capabilities, or attitudes at this point – we simply need a complete picture to start with. The details will emerge and develop after the picture is complete. Woody Allen saw this same thing when he said, "90 percent of success is simply showing up." Woody was probably talking about an individual, but this principle also applies to a team. Each team member needs to *show up* before the team can expect success. *Every single piece of the puzzle is critical, and no one piece is more important than the other... including the team leader piece.*

As the People Connection Process continues, the pieces will begin to fit more snugly together. The leader needs to understand and explain that most of the adjustments of the fit between these pieces will be performed by the team members themselves. They will understand each other's strengths and weaknesses as well, if not better, than the leader. They can then begin to make the many little adjustments that collectively add up to a significant improvement in team relationships and performance.

Expecting them to make the adjustments necessary to fit together as a team requires a high level of openness and trust. This depends almost totally on the positive environment the leader creates and the team supports. Issues with individuals can pretty much be overlooked at this point, because many of these will be swept away, or resolved by the process. Individual issues include personal conflicts, performance problems, and attitudes. Once this positive environment has been created and reinforced, then the team will grow closer together, creating a complete and tight-fitting puzzle.

> *Each team member is a piece of the puzzle, and each one is needed to complete the picture. Every single piece is critical. No one piece is more important than the other, including the team leader piece.*

NOW, LET'S GO THREE-DIMENSIONAL SO WE CAN UNDERSTAND RESONANCE.

The next important step in enabling the middle 60 percent is introducing the concept of "resonance". Resonance describes the level at which the team is working together. Resonance gets a bit difficult to describe in terms of a two-dimensional puzzle so let's go three-dimensional and transform the puzzle into a guitar. I have chosen an acoustic guitar, because it doesn't need external amplification, or help, to resonate. Can you imagine an acoustic guitar without a sound box, or neck, frets, or strings? Every one of these pieces is critical to making the guitar perform as expected. When all pieces of a guitar are present and are precisely fitted and assembled, the guitar can produce a wonderfully resonant sound.

Just as a carefully crafted guitar resonates with sound far and above what those little strings by themselves can produce, a high-performing team resonates with performance that is far and above what each team member can produce. In the real world, this resonance translates to the good feeling that everyone has at the end of the day about what they accomplished that day. They will feel like it didn't take all that much effort to be really productive. Before long, everyone will look forward to coming to work, because it's a friendly, cooperative, and productive environment. A high-performing team rates high on resonance.

Resonance is at its peak when ***all team members and leaders*** are fulfilling their roles. Resonance is so important that we need to take a closer look.

One dictionary definition of resonance is "having a prolonged, subtle, stimulating effect beyond the initial impact". A team high in resonance feels there's more driving the team than just the leader and team members. Others will describe resonance as a "finely-tuned and well-oiled machine". Cooperativeness and intensity of effort are applied to the task at hand, which encourages and excites each team member. Some people may call it team spirit, but I believe this term is much too shallow to describe it. Team spirit is more a "rah-rah" showy kind of thing, whereas resonance gets closer to the fundamental aspects of getting the job done.

Another way to describe resonance is with the term "synergy". The basic definition of synergy is that the total is greater than the sum of its individual parts. Synergy allows individuals to contribute more for a number of reasons, which we will now explore.

How does synergy work? Though I will list a number of things that can create synergy, I will let the exact definition remain as wonderfully mysterious as it has always been. Perhaps there's a division of labor, where each team member is able to do the work they are best at. Maybe the greater numbers of people have a larger pool of ideas and energy that enables goals to be reached faster. There can also be a stimulus to greater individual achievement caused by encouragement and nudges from the group. Maybe a team member's individual desire to please the group is much stronger than most might think. Whatever the mechanisms, synergy amplifies individual efforts in a well-functioning team.

The team must understand the concept of resonance and track their progress in improving it. Tracking resonance will require using a subjective measurement. Unfortunately, most managers get nervous, uneasy, and will check to see if anyone notices them taking seriously what I'm saying. They are shy of subjective measurements, because they are "not exact enough" or not politically acceptable. Subjective measurements gauge things like attitudes, which naturally appear fuzzy when a yardstick is applied to them. In spite of its fuzziness, resonance is far too important not to track, even if it has to be measured subjectively.

Many other important measurements of organization and team performance can only be measured subjectively. Dr. Deming, the architect of Japan's dramatic economic recovery after WWII, observed that the most important aspects of business cannot be measured. I believe he meant that the most important aspects of business couldn't be measured *objectively*. Many things like morale, attitude, commitment, integrity, character, and decision-making abilities, can't be measured objectively but are critical to the business. They *can be* measured subjectively, however.

The American business leaders Dr. Deming was talking to would not accept subjective measurements. They even went so far as to oversimplify the most important measurements to make them look objective. For example, I have seen leaders chosen based on their objective test scores, and not on the subjective measures of their integrity, character, and ability to connect with people. Well-defined subjective measures come closer to capturing all the relevant factors of today's world and the well-developed intuitions of our team members. They can also approximate objective measurements in their repeatability, accuracy and reliability.

Resonance is measured with the Leikert scale, a rating system designed for measuring subjective things. The Leikert scale frequently uses a scale of 1 to 5, or my favorite which is 1 to 10. For trivia buffs, Renses Likert was credited with inventing this scale in 1932 to measure attitudes and he actually used a 1 to 7 scale. You probably noticed the difference in spelling, which unfortunately, I cannot explain. If a leader takes the time to properly define resonance, and asks the team to use the Leikert scale to rate it, then a reliable, consistent, and accurate rating will result.

The team assessment tool on page 9 provides a more in-depth look at resonance, and should help significantly in defining it. It should not be surprising if the team's resonance ratings are almost identical to the team assessment scores. If they are, then the team has a good understanding of what resonance is.

> *It's important that teams understand the concept of resonance and track their progress in improving it.*

It's not possible for leaders to totally know and understand each person's performance, because leaders are oftentimes presented with images and information that are not consistent with reality. A good talker or participant in team meetings, for example, doesn't always make a good teammate. Making judgments based on appearances is a very common trap for leaders and team members as well. Team members, however, more quickly realize when they and the leader have been duped, because they spend much more time with the deceptive team member.

Leaders have many reasons to cater to the 60 percent in the middle. There's more to gain from each of them, plus they significantly outnumber the other two groups. They are hungry for good leadership, challenge, and success. Many of them will eventually step up to match the great performers in the top 20 percent, plus they have a huge positive influence on the bottom 20 percent as we shall soon see. Bad leadership can put the entire team in a bad light, but good leadership can make them all look like stars. Similar to an outstanding leader with a team, an outstanding musician can make a simple acoustic guitar sound like a million dollars.

The exact same players can look like bums, or look like stars — it all depends on leadership.

∞ CHAPTER 12: HOW ON EARTH DOES ALL THIS WORK?

"A great leader is not necessarily one who does the greatest things. He is the one who gets the people to do the greatest things."
– Ronald Reagan

THEY HAVE A SHOT AT BEING GREAT – BERKELEY PLANT STORY

People want to be significant. Some strive for it through open, loud and proud competitiveness. Others strive for significance in far quieter ways, but are just as hungry for it. Most of the working population fits into one of these two categories. The rest fit into a fringe that defies explanation. Even if they don't show it, most – if not all – of your team members want their team to excel. It's a natural need.

The People Connection fills that need in two ways. The first way is through team member participation. Participation builds ownership. People do much better with thoughts and processes they own, just as they do much better with the houses and the cars they own. The second way is through the assurance they gain from the vision. When they know where they are going, encouragement they get from their leader and from their successes is much more effective. They are also much more receptive to being held accountable for achieving the vision. Ownership builds the commitment, and the vision provides the driving force.

The immense popularity of Rick Warren's book <u>The Purpose Driven Life</u> underscores this need for significance. He calls it our "purpose". When we find it, then we have much more enthusiasm, vitality, and fulfillment in our lives.

This need for significance, or need to be great, also strongly motivates a team. This is true even under adverse circumstances. To illustrate this point, we will now visit a team who proved they were great, knowing they would be out of a job when they succeeded.

> *Participation builds ownership. People do much better with thoughts and processes they own, just as they do much better with the houses and the cars they own.*

The Berkeley Plant was scheduled to be shut down because of high manufacturing costs. The effort to outsource to Mexico and Indiana had been underway for a couple of years by the time we engaged the People Connection. Progress had been slow before the People Connection and, consequently, the plant shutdown had been delayed numerous times. The shutdown was now more than a year behind schedule.

On my first visit, it appeared their shutdown process was well planned, so I prepared to head home. All I was asked to do is to ensure the shutdown plans were solid. But then I met Ed Baker, who had some earth-shaking news. Of course, earth-shaking news is not uncommon to earthquake-prone California. Ed had just discovered that the lease stipulated a half-million dollar penalty for not vacating the facility by December 31 – and it was already November 9! Our plans were to complete this shutdown by late February or March. This new date looked absolutely impossible. Shut-downs normally drag on, not accelerate. To make matters worse, this penalty would wipe out the Berkeley Operation's profit plan for the year.

After discovering this, Thor Sorensen, the VP who headed the Berkeley Operations, and I agreed we needed to get to work immediately. Absolutely no one outside of our group thought we could save this half million dollars. This project needed the People Connection!

One by one, I made sure every staff member was crystal clear on the goal. The goal was to totally clean out the facility by the end of December.

We then talked about the specific things that would have to happen in each area to accomplish that goal. Taking one functional area (manufacturing, materials, engineering, and others) at a time, we quickly developed a plan. We made some adjustments to ensure that all the plan pieces fit together, and then got the entire team together to review it. At the end of the meeting, everyone was obviously nervous, but the vote to work the plan was unanimous.

We then met with the 48 hourly associates who remained, beginning with the union leadership. The hourly associates had been growing restless and almost hostile over the last 18 months, because of one delayed shutdown schedule after another. They were ready to move on with their lives. When we met with the union leadership, they were skeptical of our plan because of all the postponements and the ambitious nature of our plan. They soon realized that our plan was workable, and appreciated the fact we were determined to shut the plant down with grace and dignity. After thinking it through, they promptly gave the plan their full support.

We then began a series of weekly meetings with all of the hourly associates and made sure they understood the goal. At first we got pushback because of their concern that we would be shorting them their WARN (Workers Adjustment and Retraining Notification) pay. I assured them that they would not be shortchanged a single hour of pay if we closed earlier than their WARN termination date. WARN pay is the compensation the government requires an employer to pay to those affected by major lay-offs, by ensuring they have adequate notice of termination. The WARN act ensures they get paid to a certain date, even if the plant closes early. The Berkeley team quickly understood how this could work in their favor.

They actually began to get enthusiastic about the idea of closing by the end of December, and even pressed to shut it down sooner. Others asked if they could leave as soon as their departments were finished. We responded that no one would leave until all the work was complete. When their department was finished, they needed to help others finish production and clean up. No one complained and cooperation was immediate.

The WARN pay was a carrot, kind of a bonus for getting the job done early. This was an important driving force, but not the real motivator. Though important, work and pay of any amount are <u>**not**</u> something that excites people or makes them **feel significant.** They always need to feel significant, even in plant shut-downs. If not, they quickly lose their commitment and focus.

The real motivator in this shut-down story was the team's intent to prove to the world one last time how good they really were. By shutting the plant down with grace and dignity, and in a timeframe that virtually everyone outside of our team thought was impossible, they would be proving that they were the best. This goal resonated with the team.

Almost every step of the shutdown process flowed well. We said in the beginning that we would be working smarter, and not harder, to meet this aggressive schedule. Because of this, we refrained from working excess overtime, even when we lost a lot of time because of the Thanksgiving and Christmas holidays. About the first week of December everyone could see that the plant was beginning to empty.

> *The real motivator in this shut-down story was the team's intent to prove to the world one last time how good they really were.*

However, there was one serious glitch. Production orders were supposed to be shut off by then, but unfortunately that didn't happen. There was a huge, unexpected $500,000 order that was loaded into the schedule at the last minute, which threatened to destroy an already overloaded shut-down schedule.

Instead of throwing up our hands, we got the team together to reinforce the goal, and to review once again the steps required to get there. You could see panic in the eyes of some; but calmness and reason prevailed, and the plan started falling into place. The plan was as tight as any I have ever seen. The schedule was so tight, that if one team member got into trouble, then the entire plan would fail. However, we had a lot going for us: a goal, a plan, trust, accountability, and a determination to show that we were the best. We would soon see if that were enough.

As we entered the last two weeks of the year, the plant was definitely beginning to show signs of emptying, but we still had a long way to go. We didn't waste time with frequent and lengthy project meetings. The short ones we did have continued to focus on the goal and the steps to get there. We specifically avoided dwelling on problems and obstacles. Those were dealt with outside of the meetings with just the people necessary to resolve them.

I decided to leave town the last week of the shut-down to be with family for Christmas on the other side of the country. I did not make this decision lightly, but I knew that the team could function just as well without me. Whatever help they needed from me could be handled by phone. They knew the goal and how to work the plan.

Since I hadn't heard anything from them after a few days, I was overcome with curiosity. I called Ken, the acting plant manager, on December 29, and asked him how everything was going. That's when I heard those memorable words: **"production is complete and components are gone two days ahead of schedule." High morale and making the work fun were frosting on an awesome cake.** My confidence was well-founded.

To hear that morale is high and that shutdown work is fun for people who are losing their jobs the next day simply doesn't sound normal. That's because the People Connection is not normal, since so few organizations use it – so far. This Process puts an organization in high performance mode and delivers astonishing results. It's always good to hear this from more than one source, so there are two other writers that will tell you the same thing. They are Ed Oakley and Doug Krug who co-wrote the book <u>Enlightened Leadership.</u> Their observations are consistent with the case studies I have presented in this book. In essence, they are saying when people are properly led, the results are simply astonishing.

Further proof that the Berkeley Plant shut-down was exceptional was the relatively low level of workman's compensation claims. The company's past experiences with plant shutdowns always included high levels of workman's comp claims. Employees always rushed to get as much workman's comp money out of the company as they could before they lost their jobs. Many of these claims were questionable. This did not occur with the Berkeley Plant shutdown.

> *The rest of the company didn't believe they could, and were astonished at what happened. This team went above and beyond to show how much people want to be great and to be a part of something great.*

Yet another piece of evidence that the shutdown was exceptional is that relationships between management and the hourly associates were much improved. Hostility and bad attitudes were at a low level. A retirement party for a member of management was well-attended. The party coordinator remarked to me as we approached party time that she was surprised at the attitude change she had seen in the employees.

The Berkeley Plant team proved that they *still* were a great team and the best at building their products. All they needed was the opportunity to prove it, the chance to make it theirs, the "elbow-room" to make it happen, and the belief that they could do it. The rest of the company didn't believe they could, and were astonished at what happened. This team went above and beyond to show how much people want to be great and to be a part of something great.

ACCEPTANCE INCREASES

Acceptance of many things, from team decisions...to plant shutdowns...to management directives...to changes in the business environment is greatly increased with the People Connection.

A term called "buy-in" is common in team-building, and quality and productivity improvement programs. The term "buy-in", unfortunately, has become overused and abused. The original meaning of buy-in was "acceptance". However, it has now evolved into meaning a "vote". In other words, if the company wants my buy-in, then they want my vote. Companies and teams need support from team members, not votes. Although voting has its place in organizations and teams, it is generally best left for the government sector. Political processes don't apply well to producing organizations.

Creating acceptance and support for team decisions, events and management directives requires a careful orchestration of the team's discussion and an understanding of what people need.

As Stephen Covey so perceptively and eloquently states in <u>The Seven Habits of Highly Effective People,</u> people need to be heard and understood[8]. They also need to process new ideas, directives, and situations by discussing them, questioning them, having the freedom to get them wrong and learning from their mistakes. Most people and especially the "team personality" learn best by inserting some of their own personality and experiences in any new decision or directive. To make this happen, the team leader, in particular, must be vigilant about ensuring that all team members have a chance to be heard and understood by the rest of the team.

> *Companies and teams need support from team members, not votes.*

Acceptance, or buy-in, is another way of saying that new ideas, directives, and situations are understood. I have too often noticed that leaders just state the situation or directive, and since there is nothing anyone can do about it, stop the discussion right there and move on. They will almost always say that the directive was so simple that a child could understand it. That's probably true, but adults in today's complex world can't think like children. Directive leadership is depriving the team of the crucial opportunity to develop an understanding of the situation. This lack of understanding leads to a decrease in morale and team performance.

THE 60 PERCENT ARE YOUR GREATEST RESOURCE

Top team performance all hinges on the 60 percent in the middle. This was a key point in Chapter 11 and is worth repeating here. They also have an amazing impact on the bottom 20 percent.

I learned in the Foams Plant more than 20 years ago – and have watched it repeat itself unerringly since – what happens to the bottom 20 percent. After the People Connection has been operating for about a year, it becomes clear the bottom 20 percent is shrinking. The People Connection is taking care of almost all of these problem performers.

To explain how this happens, let's start with some background. One of the first responses I typically get when introducing the People Connection is how "incapable these people are". I usually hear a whole litany of examples detailing slackers, rule-breakers, and those who seem to resist the organization's purpose at every turn. Of course this happens. Any group of people, or organization, has a distribution of worker commitments and cooperativeness even if they are hand-picked. There's always a bottom 20 percent who cause 80 percent of the distractions. They are the ones who seem impossible to motivate; they complain and whine; and they regularly violate the rules. They are the ones whose behavior is commonly generalized to describe most of the organization.

Management then feels it necessary to make the rules and exercise the leadership that actually fits only the bottom 20 percent. Unfortunately, this approach leads the 60 percent to act the same way. Right-thinking leadership can get the middle 60 percent to perform like the top 20. This now turns 80 percent of the group into top performers. The choice is that simple. Unfortunately, the wrong choice has turned many teams into 80 percent poor performers.

Once the 60 percent are led to join the top 20, then the bottom 20 begins to shrink. The dynamics are surprising but understandable. The bottom 20 is a curious mix of characters who can best be sorted out by allowing the Process to run its course. For years many of these people have eluded management's attempts to fire them. They can be extremely clever and nimble in their exploits, and can rival some of the world's greatest strategic thinkers. Management doesn't have enough sound information, time, or freedom to deal effectively with them. Surprisingly, the bottom 20 percent is made up of a significant group of trouble-makers who are well worth redeeming, and the remainder are truly misfits and slackers who need to leave. The problem is that leaders can't really tell who is in which group.

> *Right-thinking leadership can get the middle 60 percent to perform like the top 20.*

Are we crazy for wanting to redeem troublemakers? Most managers warn that it's noble to want to, but it's usually a waste of time to try – and they're right. Fortunately, the People Connection does a great job of redeeming the troublemakers who can be redeemed, without any additional effort from the leader. But, why would we even want to?

The redeemed trouble-makers are usually the strongest converts and leaders. Many of them are the ones who were really trying to tell management something important. Now that they are being listened to, they follow good leadership whole heartedly.

It's at this point we encounter the most unusual twist. *The remaining misfits, poor performers, and non-redeemable trouble-makers can't stand working with the team any more and leave on their own.* Now, we could say: "That doesn't make sense. What would make them do that? Things get better for everyone during the People Connection, don't they?" The answer is "no, they only get better for those who are working to achieve the vision." The rest find it harder and more miserable than ever. If you listened to them before the People Connection, you would be led to believe that their job was barely tolerable. Just think how much worse it will be when their zealous teammates are holding them accountable for their performance.

No one is more zealous nor more intolerant than converts among the bottom 20 and middle 60 percents. In addition, they are far better able to identify the true misfits than management is. They work side-by-side with them all day long day-in and day-out. *Misfits simply can't hide from their teammates like they can the leader.* The top 20 percent don't have the same effect, because they are considered to be "goodie-goodies" and "management favorites".

This process is not perfect, but it certainly is far more effective than management can be. Whoever remains of the bottom 20 percent after the People Connection has run its course, are far easier to identify and work with. One final benefit that many leaders like is that management doesn't have to be the "bad guy" in most of these cases. Managers and leaders are like everyone else. Most of them want to be liked. Though a leader needs to deal with some hard core cases by themselves, they will be avoiding most of the gray areas where the mistakes are usually made.

I want to make one final point about the value of the middle 60 percent. I made a politically incorrect statement in a plant staff meeting one time in response to the term "these people". I had heard this countless times used derisively by almost the entire staff. This expression is far too common all over the country in many different kinds of organizations, as I have heard it said thousands of times. The term "these people" was used to describe their "laziness, their lack of education, and their lack of ability". I stated that the only difference between "these people" and the staff was the decisions they made in life. Leaders, coaches, and management, in general, tend to fall into the trap of believing they are superior to those below them in the organizational chart, in their social status, and in the pecking order.

I told the staff that college educated people worked on the production floor, because that's where they wanted to be. Mayors, teachers, community leaders, and even geniuses worked on the assembly lines. To prove me wrong would have required management to show that over the years the plant intentionally hired only the lazy, uneducated, and incapable. My argument was not well received...until something happened that opened everyone's eyes. Hard, objective data about their capabilities presented itself that proved I was right. From then on, I never heard the term "these people" again.

When management and leaders can accept that a majority of the organization has as many abilities and aptitudes as their chosen leaders and staff members, then it only makes sense to tap into that tremendous resource pool. The 20 percent on the top have always been utilized, respected and appreciated by generations of managers and supervisors. Only a few have recognized and used the tremendous potential of the middle 60 percent.

THE HUGE AMOUNT OF LOW-HANGING FRUIT

If nothing more is done than truly engage the team or workforce, then all performance measures will improve by 10 percent almost immediately. That's called "low-hanging fruit" because it's easy to get to. If the leader stays the course, then there is normally a gain of another 20 percent over the next two to three months. This happens every time the People Connection has been implemented. Once this foundation has been laid, then the proper environment has been created for Lean, Six Sigma, or any other improvement program to thrive.

> *When management and leaders can accept that a majority of the organization has as many abilities and aptitudes as their chosen leaders and staff members, then it only makes sense to tap into that tremendous resource pool.*

A lot of positive press is given to these improvement programs. They look great on paper, in theory, and in PowerPoint presentations. They claim dramatic gains in productivity, lower costs, and better service. I believe in these programs and the results they can deliver, but experience has shown that most organizations are not happy with what they do in the long run. We have all these programs with thousands of practitioners, trainers, experts, and consultants. We demonstrate remarkable progress with them. But wait awhile, and what inevitably happens is that we can't seem to hold onto the gains we've made. The People Connection fixes this problem. It's self-sustaining and creates the environment for other programs to be self-sustaining as well.

I said earlier that the People Connection can deliver 20 to 30 percent improvement without using any other program. That doesn't make it a program directly competitive with the others I've just mentioned. The People Connection is a foundation that allows the powerful tools of Lean and Six Sigma to achieve and hold onto their enormous potential. In fact, ***the People Connection is not a program at all, but rather a mindset and a meeting***.

To understand how the People Connection can deliver such gains in such a short time requires an understanding of waste and quality problems, typical of so many organizations and teams. The typical organization has a huge amount of wasted effort, wasted steps, and what is derisively called "excessive bureaucracy". The number of organizations that suffer from excessive bureaucracy can't be counted. Excessive bureaucracy leads to excessive headcount, which, unfortunately, is usually dealt with by simply cutting heads without cutting the excessive bureaucracy. The only benefit of this insanity is that it expands the market for my book. The typical organization also has many quality issues, ranging from poor service to defective products. The important thing to remember is that ***much of this waste is very apparent to many who are currently working in the middle of it***.

Lean is a program that identifies and removes this wasted time, effort, costs, and unnecessary process steps in an organization. However, team members simply need the go-ahead to eliminate the massive amounts of it they can already see. Lean tools, of course, are more effective in driving out waste in the more complex processes and over the long haul. Lean tools require the long haul because of all the time and effort involved.

Six Sigma is a program that identifies and removes the variation in processes that create quality problems. Many costs are associated with quality problems, such as rejects, scrap, rework and returns from customers. There is so much variation and so many quality issues in the typical organization that simply empowering team members to remove them will have a significant impact. Just like Lean, a basic understanding of Six Sigma concepts – and the power to do something about it – will allow a team to reduce variation and other quality problems.

Allowing the team these basic Lean and Six Sigma successes will provide them with a basic understanding of what these programs will do. What I have related on these pages about Lean and Six Sigma is enough to get a team started. This simple approach will make them hungrier for the time-consuming training and implementation of the formal improvement tools. These simple successes will also eliminate any buy-in problems, should an organization decide to mandate these programs.

TIP OF THE ICEBERG

The weekly meeting (chapter 2) has a welcome side-effect. The process that is modeled in this meeting gets used outside of the meeting as well. It essentially multiplies what the meeting accomplishes. Team members support each other's drive for the goal. They identify and act on hundreds of little steps that will help achieve the goal. Most of these steps will remain invisible, because no one feels they are significant enough to bring to the weekly meeting. However, in time, they add up to a significant amount of progress.

Also, each team member better understands and respects their role and the role of others in achieving the goals. All ideas receive more respect. All team members receive more respect. Team members will more frequently take the initiative to improve the process.

PEER PRESSURE IS FAR MORE POWERFUL THAN MANAGEMENT EXHORTATIONS

I remember Dr. Deming being death on the slogans that so often appear on walls, workplace entrances, and bulletin boards. Dr. Deming disagreed with slogans because they simply don't work.

People don't need slogans, because slogans are, too often, simple exhortations to do something that management wants, but has not provided the necessary resources or environment to accomplish. They usually end up being a good way to secretly annoy those doing the work. A slogan may be beneficial for a particular moment in the team's journey. However, most of the time they are simply going to be out of synch with the team's needs.

Peer pressure works far better than management exhortations, because it's timelier. The team is constantly growing and adjusting to daily circumstances and challenges. They are a different team every day, even if only a little. The individual team members are right in the middle of this constant growth-related change and can best understand what it will take to achieve the vision, which is fixed. They also know best what to expect from each other every single day.

Peer pressure is more powerful than management exhortations, because of the nature of its accountability. We can all remember those days when we couldn't get it together or couldn't complete a project. We usually felt worse about letting our team down than our boss. Our peers are in a much better position to see, understand, and appreciate our performance, or lack of it. Most team members feel the greatest accountability and commitment to the team and to each other.

We usually felt worse about letting our team down than our boss.

PEOPLE CONNECTION SUCCESS WHETS THE APPETITE FOR MORE POWERFUL TOOLS

A series of small successes in reducing waste and variation lays the foundation for success with the powerful tools of Lean and Six Sigma. Once your team begins the continuous improvement journey, they will continue pushing the envelope. They will eventually exhaust the low-hanging fruit and will look for ways to solve the more difficult waste and quality problems in the organization. They will naturally be requesting training in these tools.

Training is one of the most popular items on team wish lists. People typically enjoy learning more about what they're good at. Since the low-hanging fruit is a good confidence builder, than Lean and Six Sigma should be popular and beneficial classes.

ALL DECISIONS ARE NOW POINTED IN THE SAME DIRECTION

There are too many decisions made by every team member every day for leaders to directly control. Leaders and managers must remove themselves from direct control, and instead influence these decisions through the People Connection. Establishing and maintaining a clear vision and engaging the team in achieving it is by far the most effective way to do that.

When differences in team member's agendas exist, it's fairly obvious that the team will perform poorly. What's not so obvious is the performance degradation that occurs when team members *agree* on the same vision, but differ in their understanding of it – even if only slightly. Usually, no open conflict arises when these unseen differences occur, but there's a significant loss of performance anyway. Decisions are influenced heavily by a person's understanding, and most team member decisions are made from a number of different choices. These choices usually range from worst to best. Decisions pointed in different directions work against one another, instead of working harmoniously and synergistically together.

For example, one team member may understand the vision as being the best company in the industry at pleasing the customer. Another team member may understand the vision as being the *most effective company* in the industry at pleasing the customer. The first team member will be driven to please the customer even at a loss to the company. The second team member will be driven to be the best at pleasing the customer only if there is also profit to the company. If there is no profit, there is no company, and therefore no customers to please. The People Connection will ensure that these fine distinctions in vision and understanding are clearly understood by all team members.

UNDERSTANDING AND MASTERING THE PROCESS

This is the last of three sections in this book. The interest that has carried you this far is commendable. The more you digest of this book, the greater your team's excitement and effectiveness.

This section will lead to process mastery. As in the other two sections, this is not a textbook of tools. Other than the two little tools I felt necessary to add, I avoided all others because they so often detract from what the Process is all about, and that is people. This book is all about mindset and a meeting, not tools. Mastering the Process is all about mastering how we relate to people in a team environment. Though this book is practical in application, it must also get deep inside our thought processes and show us how to change the way we think. I believe you will find this experience exciting and rewarding.

∞CHAPTER 13: HOW DID THE PEOPLE CONNECTION BECOME SO POWERFUL?

"Leadership is the ability to hide your panic from others."
– Anonymous

THE POWER OF A NEW PARADIGM

Leaders need to understand that the difference between what their teams should be, and what they are, is primarily due to their own thinking. What leaders think about people, and the many problems facing their team, has a dramatic impact on how the organization or team actually works. In most cases, leaders are oblivious to how their thinking is impacting those who are doing the job. If a leader thinks their team is full of bozos, then the team will act like bozos. Faulty thinking impacts decisions and how they are carried out in such subtle ways that they're almost impossible to detect, *except by those doing the work impacted by those decisions.*

Changing how we think may be very difficult for some. For many others, however, the People Connection offers a refreshing new way to think that better fits today's realities. Conventional team-building efforts, which often include replacing team members and/or replacing the leader aren't nearly as effective as a right thinking leader. A leader who adopts the People Connection will be successful almost all of the time.

EXTREME NEED IS THE MOTHER OF REFINEMENT

The principles in this book were discovered, developed, and refined under a series of severe tests. It's probably more accurate to say "re-discovered", since they are not really new. The advantage of this "refinement by fire" is that these principles are "fat-free". They are not complicated. The People Connection is a good example of lean and mean. One of the severest tests the People Connection withstood was the outsourcing of the Decatur facility.

> *Leaders need to understand that the difference between what their team should be, and what they are, is primarily due to their own thinking.*

We were never able to resolve the component supply problem for the Decatur facility, which unfortunately contributed to its shutdown. Our suppliers held our business with low prices and were not held sufficiently accountable for service because of the different goals of Central Sourcing and the plants. The Decatur plant staff understood the solution, but couldn't get management to accept it. Top management held Central Sourcing responsible for prices and the plants responsible for service. The Decatur plant wanted authority to discipline suppliers for service problems but was not able to get it. Low prices alone were sufficient for a supplier to retain our business. The only consolation was that other plants were experiencing the same problems as Decatur, although, fortunately for them, not as bad.

When credible rumors about a pending shutdown decision reached our plant, we put together a 30-page white paper analyzing the most advisable strategy. This proposal would have resulted in substantial cost savings. High volume products such as simple emergency exit lights weren't costly to make. Very low volume products such as complex control systems required skill and expertise that weren't easy to transfer to contract manufacturers. Medium volume products, however, required enough labor to justify outsourcing them to a lower cost supplier. We recommended outsourcing the medium volume products but not the high volume and very low volume products.

The recommendation to keep Decatur open met with a lot of resistance. It was impossible, some thought, for Decatur to pay $11.50 per hour and be competitive with the Chinese at 60 cents per hour. We pointed out in our white paper that our labor content was a relatively low 15 percent (materials made up the remaining 85 percent). Contract manufacturer profit margins were typically 12 percent, and there was an abundance of hidden costs such as additional freight and higher inventories. Material costs would remain pretty much the same in China. We would end up paying 12 percent of this 15 percent labor component for contractor profits. This would leave only three percent to pay for contract labor and hidden costs. Even though we eventually convinced Finance that we were right, we still lost our case in the end.

One major factor that led to this wrong decision was the standard cost system. The standard cost system assigns labor and materials that can be directly linked to the manufacture of a product to that very product. All other costs (such as set up and changeover costs and any inefficiencies due to other causes) are lumped together into one pool, which is divided equally among all products. This improperly burdens high volume products, which are typically the cheapest to make because they don't require as many setups and as much material handling. In other words, much of the higher costs of producing short production runs are "averaged into" the costs of producing the high volume products. As you can see, standard costing is very similar to average costing.

To prove the validity of our financial analysis, we quoted a handful of high volume products that a Chinese supplier was quoting on. Using the standard cost system, our books showed a cost savings of $2.5 million by having China build them for us. Using our system of actual cost (Activity Based Costing), we showed there was only a $300,000 savings by having China build them. What we didn't realize is that we had overlooked some hidden costs, which were subsequently discovered by our Finance people.

A couple of financial VP's confided in me much later that our white paper claims were in fact correct, and that it was a mistake to shut down the Decatur facility. Cost savings the company had hoped to realize from the lower labor rates in China never materialized.

What finally clinched the outsourcing decision was the arrival of a consultant hired to help the company revamp the entire manufacturing network (which involved all plants including Decatur), and again the great disparity between Chinese and Decatur labor rates came up. This time opinions again focused on labor rates, rather than on a full financial analysis, which resulted in the decision to outsource the facility. China's low labor rate trumped all reason.

Outsourcing Decatur was an almost impossible feat. In all of our research, we have never found an outsourcing project that involved as much complexity and scale as this one did. We had approximately 25,000 unique products and enough work to employ 275 people in a full production mode. Approximately 25,000 tasks had to be performed to complete the job. We had to outsource to companies who, in most cases, lacked the full capabilities to produce our products, so we had to train them. We accomplished all of this in a little over a year with no extra help for either Decatur or the receiving facilities. Decatur also had to help build the production capabilities for our suppliers and continue to provide good service for the products remaining in Decatur. Because of system constraints, products could not be produced simultaneously by Decatur and the contract manufacturers. Every product move had to be in full production almost immediately.

Our team included the entire group of people at both Decatur and the contract manufacturers who were assimilating these products. This team numbered from 100 to 150 people. Though there were ample opportunities for friction and discord because of the intense pressures and complications of these transfers, the process flowed smoothly.

In our weekly meetings, I kept the entire team focused on the objective and what it was going to take to reach it. There was little, if any time, available to address problems, complaints and disagreements. When these came up, we would refocus and split off into much smaller task forces to address the few issues that survived the refocus. This process worked very well, given that our weekly meetings were large and never went over an hour. We felt very bad about shutting a plant down, but we all felt good about what we had accomplished and how well our team worked together. A key leader from one of the contract manufacturers even complimented our project by saying that it was publishable.

I could not have succeeded as the leader of this project without the People Connection. The entire team was under intense pressure for two years, counting the extensive preparation time. A tremendous amount of coordination was required between seven different facilities and about 150 different people. Tens of thousands of tasks had to be completed, with many impossible deadlines and obstacles. The workload was nearly crushing for everyone involved. And yet...there were no casualties. Not one person crashed.

The team clearly understood that failure simply was not an option, because the fall-out would be so severe. We would not be able to reverse the process, since we were in essence burning the bridges behind us. We had to believe we would succeed. Regardless of the setbacks or obstacles that came up, we never hesitated to jump into working a way around or through them. I believe this kind of thinking profoundly drives performance. I am convinced that if I, personally, didn't believe in the team, they would have detected it, and that would have caused the project to fail. We were so close to the edge for two years that a simple weakness in thinking would have led to failure.

A leader cannot hide what they think about their team. For example, management can be frustrated and disappointed with their team and carefully avoid any word of it, but the people doing the work will still detect what they're thinking. Decisions that seem so objective and straightforward to decision-makers will carry with them all kinds of messages that are invisible to management. But these messages are like blaring loudspeakers to those doing the work. Communications are more than the written and spoken words. The context – even the decisions that weren't made and the words that weren't said – communicate volumes.

Although I cannot fully explain how workers can "read the minds" of management, I can say that decision-making is much more complex than most people realize. Even the simplest decisions package a whole lot of meaning that can be deciphered by clever and insightful team members.

Simple decisions are really very complex, and the people doing the work can see that. They can clearly understand most, if not all, of the factors that should have gone into making the decision, and therefore can easily reconstruct the decision-making process. The unfortunate result is that the leaders don't have a clue that they have communicated anything negative, but they can see the decline in team performance. A team who is not focused on a solid vision will constantly look for clues hidden in decisions so it can better understand its leaders and how they feel about them.

THE PEOPLE CONNECTION FOCUSES ON FOUR ESSENTIAL PRINCIPLES

It is important to memorize these four simple principles:

1. *People want to be great and to be a part of something great.* All leaders have to do is *make it possible* for people to be great and leaders will win the heart and soul of the team.
2. *Every team has a lot of waste due to process variation, which is the **root of quality problems and customer dissatisfaction**.*
3. *Every team has a lot of waste due to process design. There is a lot of effort that is not necessary.*

4. *Every leader has blind spots – A team leader or a team member cannot see everything that is going on. Leaders and team members alike need to trust and rely on one another to fill in the blind spots.*

These four simple principles need to be fully engrained in the mindset of the leader and of the team. Don't add sophistication to your initiatives or programs until the mindset change is engrained and the team is consistently performing in a superior fashion.

The most critical thing to remember and believe about people is that "People want to be great and to be a part of something great". Every person in the organization has both good and bad qualities, no matter what their standing or position. That is just the way we are. Understanding how to tap the good qualities and fully employ them is critical to a leader. Trying to deal with the bad qualities is largely a waste of time. Focus on the good qualities and the *influence* of the bad qualities will shrink.

There's no motivation like the self-motivation that people show when they believe they can accomplish great things. I have seen people cancel their time-off so they can work on team projects. They will work energetically and intensely on problems they have taken ownership of until they find a solution – come hell or high water. The goal becomes their obsession and most of the problems and frustrations they have dealt with in the past will become insignificant. Beware of the cynics. The countless negative examples they come up with, even if they are real, are more than overshadowed by the good that comes out of tapping into the good side of people in the organization.

The second principle leads us to Six Sigma. Six Sigma basically is a mindset for removing variation from the process. Variation creates waste, rejects and customer dissatisfaction. Six Sigma features many excellent tools and processes, but these are most effectively learned and applied by a team who already has experience with reducing variation. The People

Connection provides this experience and a fundamental understanding of why it's important.

Six Sigma tools are simply tools; they cannot solve an organization's problems by themselves. They are powerful, but if removing variation isn't instilled into the culture to begin with, then they won't deliver lasting results. Failure to instill Six Sigma principles into the culture will allow it to degenerate into a tool of a select few who demonstrate significant but short-lived improvements.

The third principle leads us to Lean. The two critical things to remember about Lean are that it is single piece flow and the methodology for removing waste from the process. Similar to Six Sigma, Lean has many excellent tools that lead to waste reduction. Also similar to Six Sigma, these tools are not going to achieve lasting results if Lean thinking is not instilled into the organization.

Single piece flow is a radical change in thinking when it comes to work moving through multiple process steps. Our collective conditioning and instinct is to get very efficient at processing a batch before moving it to the next step. The problem with batch processing, however, is that it creates extensive waste. It's wasteful because there's more inventory in the process to support efficient batch processing, plus there is more likelihood of waste due to quality problems. If a quality problem occurs there's more to rework. Quality problems are discovered immediately with single-piece flow, and the single piece is all that has to be reworked.

I have actually seen, on many occasions, that the improvements made by focusing on these four simple principles far surpass the improvements achieved by using the Lean and Six Sigma tools in a culture that isn't ready for them. An incredible amount of waste and variation occurs in most processes that properly engaged people can remove on the spot, quietly and almost invisibly. As quiet and invisible as these little improvements are, they collectively will display themselves prominently on the bottom line.

The first three principles speak to how the leader and the team are to approach their work and one another. The fourth principle addresses how leaders see their world. What a leader can see is critical. A leader who is wearing blinders is short-changing the team. Leaders need to expand their perspective, or what they can see, by relying on others to fill in their blind spots.

Leaders must conduct a thorough, continuous examination and re-examination of the thought processes and decisions of the team as an entity, the individual team members, and themselves. They need to listen carefully and give thoughtful consideration to the perspectives of others. We all have blind spots that someone, somewhere can shed light on.

We really understand the new paradigm when we internalize a new and positive belief in, and understanding of, people; a drive to remove waste; a drive to remove variation from our processes; and a reliance on what others can see and perceive that we cannot. These four principles need to be an integral part of our everyday thinking. Once we have this, nothing revealed in our decisions will compromise the performance of our teams.

THE REAL POWER OF THE NEW PARADIGM

These four principles are sufficient to create improvements of 20 to 30 percent organization wide. Once top management has adopted this new paradigm, they suddenly discover they have a new ground-swell of support. When the 80 percent who want to leave their jobs (according to the statistics) are provided the opportunity to buy into the goal and the process, and can see that success is possible, then it will appear that anything is possible. People truly want to help achieve success for the organization.

Most problems in business are not so complicated that only management can understand them. In fact, most problems in business *seem* complicated, because so much of the business remains "hidden" from management. It's invisible because they haven't tapped into the knowledge, the creativity, and the insight that the workforce is more than willing to share. A business becomes much simpler when management listens.

Tom Paterson, a Nobel Laureate and one of the most brilliant business thinkers and practitioners of our time, has estimated that a typical organization only uses about 5 percent of a team's capacity. This says that teams can improve their capacity by 20 times! Even if the team is really at 25 percent, then it is no wonder team performance improvements appear astonishing.

Tom Paterson was recognized as a master strategist by many Fortune 100 leadership teams, and the most effective strategic facilitator of his time by Peter Drucker, one of the 20th century's best known management theorists and authors. Tom Paterson not only knew what it took to develop a powerful strategic plan, but also how to get it implemented.

Managers make a big mistake when they feel that it is up to them to ensure that improvements are implemented. What really adds to the power of an organization is empowering the workforce to make the improvements that they have jointly agreed upon. This is especially true when the ideas came from the workforce to begin with. Even "less-than-best" ideas from the workforce will out-perform better ideas from other sources, because their heart, soul, and pride are in those ideas and in making them work.

When leadership's thinking is right, and the vision throughout the organization is in alignment, then the power that arises is sufficient to drive any organization to the top. Organizations or teams who achieve this success are not benefiting from "good chemistry". They are experiencing alignment in thinking and goals. A like-minded team is thrilling to watch.

> *There is no business so mundane or boring that it can overshadow the brilliance of a turned-on team.*

To emphasize the above quote, just ask yourself why people come from all over the world to visit something as mundane as a fish market. This team of about 20 people has impressed the world with their brilliant performances. They have achieved enviable business success, and have captivated countless customers and audiences with their inspiring attitudes, their ability to connect with others, and throwing fish around the market. The world famous Pike Place Fish Market in Seattle is an example of what a team can do with something like the People Connection.

> We never know how high we are
> Till we are called to rise;
> And then, if we are true to plan,
> Our statures touch the skies.
> – Emily Dickinson, Poet

∞CHAPTER 14: SHARPLY FOCUSING ALL THAT POWER

"The great leaders are like the best conductors — they reach beyond the notes to reach the magic of the players."
— Blaine Lee

LET'S GET REAL ABOUT MANAGEMENT CONTROL OVER DECISION-MAKING

Thousands of decisions are made every day by teams. Most managers would prefer that a select group of brilliant people make each of these decisions, but that's not physically possible. The sheer volume necessitates that most of these get made by team members who, unfortunately, usually don't think the way management wants. Decisions such as the acceptability of a product, how to "bend" a company rule, or how to deal with a problem customer are some examples.

Another challenge occurs when management decisions become directives. Interpretations can vary widely depending on each team member's understanding of the vision and goals. A person who believes the company's goal of winning the trophy means getting a bonus will very likely behave differently, and less desirably, from the one who believes that winning the trophy means being the best at creating and maintaining happy customers. Both support the directive to win the trophy, but each one will carry it out differently.

Both of these challenges are best addressed by influencing the team, not directing it. Controlling a team by micromanaging or directing without their involvement does not produce superior results. *Management control of decision-making and star team performances are mutually exclusive — we can't have both.*

I was surprised to discover how decision-making works in a union facility. I had heard many warnings about how difficult it is to work with a union. However, union facilities can actually be a *plus*. *Please understand that I neither advocate nor condemn unions.* They can abuse power as well as management can. Union facilities have an advantage because they already have some valuable experience in joint decision-making and organization. This is due to their participation in developing and enforcing contracts. Unions can be a big help in the change process, but only if they have the right paradigm.

The Conyers Plant illustrates how well management and the union can work together.

> *Management control of decision-making and star team performances are mutually exclusive – we can't have both.*

THE CONYERS PLANT

As a reminder, this plant had been a troubled plant for many years and had gone through years of downsizing. Most of this was due to chronic poor relationships between union and management. However, both the union and the plant now had new leadership.

We did many bold things to turn this facility around. Efficiencies were poor, costs were high, and quality was low. The contract had grown to absurd proportions and created so much inflexibility that it was nearly impossible to operate efficiently and effectively. An entitlement mentality essentially blocked any changes that caused discomfort or disruption for anyone. The first thing that Jack Anderson, our new VP of Manufacturing, did was demand a totally new contract...and got it.

This new contract gave us the flexibility that we needed to survive, but it turned the team members' world upside down. Many had jobs for years they weren't qualified for, because they were protected by the contract. The new contract took away all of their old jobs, and everyone had to qualify for the new ones. Those who couldn't read or write faced serious difficulties, since most of the new jobs required literacy skills.

The team members rose to the occasion, and though there were some sad failures, there were many great individual, as well as team, accomplishments. The plant began to move forward in earnest. The company provided verbal and math literacy classes that were well-attended and the people worked hard at bettering their skills. We spent a lot of time working with our team members in getting them focused on the goal and the efforts to get there.

Jack was moved on to managing multiple plants, and Cedric Hayes was named as his replacement. I was assigned to the position of Fabrication Manager reporting to Cedric. Fabrication was a troubled department. Within a week or two of taking over this department, we were producing at a 10 percent higher rate. My predecessor, by the way, was one of the managers who had always degradingly called his group "these people". He was smart enough to hide his words from them, but he could not hide his thoughts, as no one can.

One day we had to move people from one shift to another to balance our crews and skills after a recent downsizing. We had one lead operator who resisted the move to day shift. An old clause in the new contract protected him, if we interpreted it the old way, but would force him to move if we interpreted it in the *spirit* of the new contract. He filed a grievance against the move. I anticipated a battle.

The scene now turns to a meeting between the lead operator, his union steward, the chairman of the local chapter of the union, and me. I fully expected to be outnumbered in this battle, but I was an amazed observer rather than a combatant. The lead operator stated his case to Jan Marshall, his union steward, and Lewis Hall his union chairman. I allowed Jan and Lewis to comment before I presented my case. Much to my surprise, they both turned immediately to the lead operator. They told him that the situation was now different.

They explained that the survival of the plant was at stake, and many people had to make changes that were uncomfortable. These changes were necessary and, in most cases were eventually embraced by those who made them. They asserted that the lead operator had no cause for a grievance and simply needed to make the move. Incidents like this one occurred with increasing frequency.

We were winning more and more converts in our struggle for survival. Lewis, the union chairman, actually stopped me one day and said: "When you, Jack, and Cedric said your goal was to save the plant, nobody believed you at first. It's now clear that you and many others are working hard to make that happen. There are few resisters left, and everyone else is working as hard as I have ever seen them to save this facility." These comments are particularly meaningful given that Lewis was once regarded by management as a radical. Our performance was quickly improving. Our productivity was almost 50 percent higher than when we started. Quality costs had dropped by more than 90 percent. Morale was very high.

HOW TO PUT AFTERBURNERS ON YOUR TEAM

Having everyone understand thoroughly what the goal is – and the actions needed to get there – has a synergistic effect. It also provides team members with a high level of confidence in their leaders and their own abilities. They are more willing to fully commit themselves in an environment they can trust.

Figure 14A shows two teams, each with 20 members. Imagine each arrow as representing a team member and the direction they are heading.

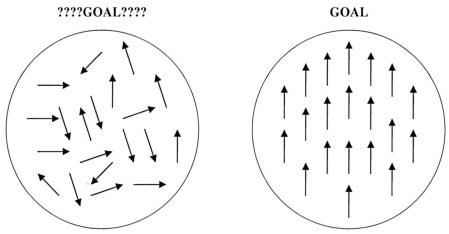

Figure 14A. The left diagram shows a team as they naturally exist. The right diagram shows a team that has been aligned with the goal immediately above them.

There's no way to tell of course, which direction the team is heading in the left diagram. They are working against themselves, canceling out the efforts of those working in the opposite direction. The team on the right has far more power.

The one on the left is the natural state of affairs for most teams. Accept it as it is and provide a clear vision of the goal and team members will gladly realign themselves.

The team on the right represents a team "on afterburners". Afterburners, as you probably know, give jet engines a tremendous boost of power. We are so used to working in teams like the one on the left, that only the "awesome" and "astonishing" words best describe the one on the right. I hope that someday the one on the right will be the norm, and that I will have to stop using superlatives. I can't wait.

A single meeting that creates a crystal clear direction just doesn't happen. One is never enough, even if it lasts all day. Though human failings contribute significantly to this problem, the largest part of it is because people simply don't see even the "most obvious" things in the same way. The visioning process is a delicate journey that has to be ongoing for weeks, perhaps months, before it's clear to everyone. ***Getting everyone on the same page depends more on the <u>number of meetings over a period of time</u> than the length of the meeting(s).***

One of Dr. Deming's 14 Points is the "Constancy of Purpose". You may recall Dr. Deming as the architect of Japan's dramatic economic recovery after WWII. His 14th Point[9] addresses our problem. It says in essence that we must keep driving in the same direction for a long time to get everyone truly on board.

One bad management habit that is all too common today is to constantly change directions. Management often changes directions every two to six months because the previous one "wasn't working". These directions are typically introduced as exciting new programs, or initiatives, and are cynically labeled as "the flavor of the month" by team members. This habit actually compounds the problems that management was trying to solve.

Getting everyone on the same page depends more on the number of meetings over a period of time than the length of the meeting(s).

Of course, the reason for any new program, or initiative, is well-intentioned. However, most of these new programs overlook the needs of the team. Though team members will almost always provide their support out of a sense of duty and/or fear, they will also know instinctively when such programs are missing the mark. If they have seen a lot of them, then they frequently become hardened cynics who can predict precisely the struggle and demise of the program.

Expecting improved behaviors from the new program without also addressing the teams' needs, communicates a lack of respect for the team and a sense that management doesn't know what they're doing. Requiring team members to embrace a "flavor of the month", and shoulder the responsibility for its success, is an insult to the team who is fully aware of its fatal flaws.

It's no wonder that team members get numb and wish they could find another job. All those "flavors" oftentimes disengage an increasing number of team members so subtly, that management has to look close and listen carefully to see it. Weakened performance is usually the only clue of a team whose needs have not been met.

Leaders need to carefully develop a vision that will withstand the test of time…and the most probable of circumstances. They then need to carefully communicate that vision, taking the weeks or months that are required. A carefully developed and communicated vision should be in place for years.

THE HUMAN POWERHOUSE

There is something about a resonating team that is very impressive and compelling. People who watch them say things like "this is huge! I am blown away!" and "on a scale of 1 to 10 you walk the talk at an 11!" In 22 years my enthusiasm for working with teams has increased instead of grown old. I never cease to be amazed at what they can do, nor how seemingly without great effort these astounding performances blossom.

WHAT ARE PEOPLE REALLY ABOUT?

There's one key driving principle that makes all the rest of the People Connection possible. This principle is: *people want to be great and to be a part of something great.* When management makes that possible, then people will 1) run through walls, 2) leap up and over cliffs, and 3) scale tall buildings to accomplish their goals. *The purest and most powerful form of motivation is when people can truly connect with the opportunity to be great and to be a part of something great.*

The first thing I hear from managers when I make this audacious assertion is they have too many 1) slackers, 2) rule-breakers, 3) people who won't commit themselves, and 4) those who seem to work or conspire against the organization's purpose. This is a self-defeating excuse. Any group of people has a varied distribution of team members, even if they are hand-picked. The 20 percent on the bottom will always be there. The 60 percent in the middle hold the key.

There are two kinds of motivation: intrinsic and extrinsic. Intrinsic motivation has far more power than extrinsic. Intrinsic motivation comes from within. *The opportunity to be great and to be a part of something great is a powerful intrinsic motivator.* Extrinsic motivation is the motivation that comes from outside the person. The fear of losing a job is an extrinsic motivation to work conscientiously. The prospect of a bonus is extrinsic motivation to work harder. One of management's favorites, "a swift kick in the pants" is extrinsic motivation. Extrinsic motivation is short-lived, whereas intrinsic is long-lasting.

The purest and most powerful form of motivation is when people can truly connect with the opportunity to be great and to be a part of something great.

Extrinsic motivators don't last because they don't address the core needs of people. They do have an important role to play, however. A high-performing team also requires the essential extrinsic motivators such as competitive pay and recognition.

Let's hear what tennis champion Chris Evert has to say. "The great high of winning Wimbledon lasts for about a week. You go down in the record books, but you don't have anything tangible to hold on to." The intrinsic motivation to become great was far more effective and long-lasting than the extrinsic motivation of the Wimbledon itself.

Whatever the high-performing team's final intrinsic and extrinsic motivation balance turns out to be, there is absolutely no substitution for intrinsic. Intrinsic motivation provides the high octane fuel for outstanding team performance. Most managers place far too much importance on extrinsic motivators, and almost totally ignore intrinsic. Intrinsic motivation is truly the "hard stuff" that Tom Malone from Milliken was referring to.

CONYERS CHURCH

My wife and I were looking for a church some years ago, and we seemed to be making a good connection with the Conyers Church. I distinctly remember one day at lunch with the pastor, Nat Johnson. He expressed serious concern about the future of his congregation. He observed that it was aging, unable to attract younger people, and not engaged. All of this sounded like something the People Connection could address, so I expressed confidence the situation could be improved.

My offer to help Nat got lost in the shuffle over the next several months. Part of that shuffle was a program called "Vision 2000". It was an effort on the part of the larger church organization to reinvigorate the local churches.

As a part of this effort, my wife, Lynn, and I were invited to visit Fraser Church, which was very successful. A group from our church spent a day there that involved a significant amount of time with their pastor. Their church was vigorous, successful, and growing rapidly. I was amazed how similar the Fraser model was to the People Connection. The principles, the approach, and the values were all the same. I excitedly informed our group that this was exactly what I did in the business world, so I knew how to make it work.

When we got back home, my comment reached Nat's ears, and he asked me to take a larger role in the Vision 2000 effort. We loosely followed the process provided by the larger church organization, but primarily focused on using the People Connection. What we learned about vision, surveys, and small group working sessions from the Vision 2000 program have been invaluable enhancements to the People Connection.

We first focused on the vision itself. We had a meeting with the entire congregation to explain what the Vision 2000 process was, and why they were an essential part of it. To help communicate what we were doing, we performed a skit. One thing that came out in this skit is a verse from the Bible that states, "where the people lack vision they will perish", which resonated with the congregation. We stressed that a dialogue about the vision was important. Since the congregation was too large for a single dialogue, we divided into small groups.

The congregation was excited. To give the small groups the material they needed, we asked the congregation to fill out a survey regarding the church and its vision. We were surprised to achieve a 90 percent response rate, where 10 percent is more typical.

There were resisters, however. The senior adults made it very clear they were happy with the church the way it was, and did not want it to change. The Vision 2000 Committee responded that no changes would be made that were inconsistent with the vision of the church, and without the full support of the entire church body, including them. Their response surprised everyone.

At first, there was a lot of worry about the time required for the small group meetings, but then the momentum began to build as more and more groups agreed to get together for the prescribed four weekly meetings. Discussions were rich, and enthusiasm was high. This enthusiasm and commitment spilled over into many other areas within the church. Pledging the budget was much easier than normal, and it was a record budget.

People were stepping forward at a much higher rate than usual to fill volunteer positions in the church organization.

The surprising thing about the seniors is that they, too, began meeting in small groups and participating whole-heartedly in the Vision 2000 effort. This group had a long-standing reputation for being resistant to change. In fact, they were so enthusiastic that they didn't stop their small group meetings after the prescribed four. They kept on meeting for many months discussing how the church could be reinvigorated.

The church was fired up, and everyone noticed it. We began attracting more visitors. We also reached out to other churches doing similar things to see what we could learn. Several delegations went to the progressive and highly respected Willow Church to get new ideas. The Conyers Church changed radically in a short period of time.

HOW DO WE REALLY ENGAGE PEOPLE?

"We need better communications" is a tired and worn-out phrase. However, it is still essential in engaging people. Unfortunately, that generally gets interpreted as talk more, write more, and polish presentations. But, how many times in long meetings do participants wipe their weary brows and wonder where they are and where they're going. Long meetings are usually a waste of time because they are too much to absorb. Short meetings (one hour) with focused, concise, and consistent communications with a purpose work, by far, the best. Regularity is more valuable in gaining full alignment and engagement than long meetings.

> *Long meetings are usually a waste of time because they are too much to absorb. Short meetings (one hour) with focused, concise, and consistent communications with a purpose work, by far, the best.*

Today's short attention spans don't mix well with long meetings. We have too many other demands on our time, such as cell phones, emails, and other meetings. I once read that trainers need to understand that people can learn only one new thing per day. Even if the real number is higher than that, my experience says that it isn't much higher.

Structured and efficient communication is essential, but there is also another essential element. Stephen Covey in his book the <u>Seven Habits of Highly Effective People</u> states that one of the Habits is "to seek first to understand then to be understood"[10]. This is a crucial practice in engaging any team. This practice promotes buy-in, which is essential for full engagement.

Team members must have an opportunity to "bend, fold, spindle, and mutilate" the decision, or topic, under discussion. Though this might be unnerving to many managers and leaders, allowing the team to do this means they can better learn: 1) how it works, 2) why it works, and 3) how decisions are made. Though many managers interpret this as resistance, they stand to learn as much from this practice as the team. Wise leaders will also allow team members an opportunity to influence as much as possible the decisions that must be handed to them. This ensures a much stronger buy-in from the group.

Team leaders who take this risk will feel vulnerable because they might look slow in front of the team. That's hard, but it's okay to struggle in front of the group. This struggle will increase our leadership bank account balance instead of reducing it – so don't hesitate to say "I don't understand". When we do understand, then it's important to prove we do by paraphrasing the points made and ask for corrections. The leaders then need to *act* in ways that are consistent with their new understanding.

After the leaders act, they need to seek feedback, both one-on-one and in group settings. Leaders need not fear talking to the "rabble-rousers" and "trouble-makers"; sometimes they are the best barometers for what the team is really thinking. They are not shy, and it's often surprising how helpful they can be. Never belittle anyone's comments or ideas in the meeting; treat every remark with respect. The team is watching closely how the leader reacts to the trouble-makers. The 60 percent in the middle, in particular, will interpret these responses as applying to them, also. Our focus should be on the 60 percent.

The team will not become fully engaged until they truly feel they and their contributions are respected. The leader doesn't even have to like their ideas, and if the right environment has been created, then the leader's dislikes won't stop the team from making the right decisions. It is also important for the leader to ensure that ideas from each team member get treated respectfully by all the others. Those ideas selected by the group for implementation must be implemented if full engagement is to be maintained.

∞CHAPTER 15: PERSEVERE, PERSEVERE, PERSEVERE!

"A good leader inspires others with confidence in him; a great leader inspires them with confidence in themselves."
– Unknown

HOW TO PERSEVERE AND WHY WE MUST

The People Connection's primary resource requirement is *perseverance.* Perseverance separates those who will succeed from those who won't. A tree can grow faster with an abundance of water and fertilizer; so can teams. However, both still grow with what seems like glacial slowness. But if we're patient, we'll be struck at how much both the tree and the team have grown. We can over-water and over-fertilize the tree and end up killing it; the same happens with teams. Patience and perseverance are critical.

Many developmental activities go on behind the scenes that are almost impossible to see. These activities require calendar time. Consider the way that ducks swim. They seem to move without effort; but under the surface of the water, those feet can be churning furiously. Likewise, a team develops furiously below the waterline even though they seem to be just cruising effortlessly along.

UNDERSTANDING ORGANIZATIONAL INERTIA... AND MOMENTUM

Creating a common understanding and interpretation of the goal takes a lot of time, effort, and regular repetition. Many events are often necessary to reveal and reconcile the differences in thinking about the vision.

Unfortunately, this is commonly interpreted as resistance. However, momentum begins to build as more and more people "get it". Once the critical mass gets it, then the momentum becomes hard to stop or redirect.

Difficulty in building momentum or changing directions is what we call "inertia". This is not a matter of team member ability, intelligence or commitment; it simply takes time.

One of Dr. W. Edward Deming's 14 Points was "to stay the course". As one of the world's foremost quality gurus, he wrote the 14 Points to help transform American Industry. The first of his 14 Points addresses organizational inertia. American managers are notoriously impatient. They are usually focused on showing good bottom-line results every quarter, instead of doing the right things for the longer term. If managers were patient in doing the right things, then the quarterly results would actually improve more quickly in the long run. "Staying the course" is just another way of saying "persevere".

I will address all of Dr. Deming's 14 Points to show how similar they are to the People Connection. However, let's get to know Dr. Deming a little better first.

I attended a couple of Dr. Deming's four-day seminars and was impressed with his intensity, his insight, his mental powers, and his dedication, even at 94 years of age. Although, physically, he required some assistance getting on and off the stage, he was more than capable in debates and dialogues. He was a formidable and nimble adversary in a debate, and I never saw anyone come close to bettering him. He welcomed these challenges because he said we were all there to learn, including him.

Dr. Deming was a man of tremendous influence. His style was direct, crusty and confrontational, but you could tell he had a heart of gold. He was highly critical of typical management practices, blaming them for 80 percent of all the problems in industry today. In spite of his criticisms, American managers were drawn to him. His seminars were always full. Four to five hundred people per seminar was not unusual. He was methodical and actually read from the seminar workbook page by page. It sounds boring, but after the first day you could see its remarkable effect on the crowd, including my boss, who attended two of them with me. Dr. Deming's seminars were mind-changing.

Each participant in these seminars received a number of Dr. Deming's books, one of which was <u>Out of the Crisis.</u> This book was his most important and popular work. At each break, most attendees, including me, tried to get him to autograph their copy. I finally got his signature and was blown away by what he told me as he was signing my book.

Many breaks throughout the day were often taken up by presentations honoring Dr. Deming. They had to be done during break, since he did not allow any distractions from valuable seminar time. Just before he signed my book, there was a particularly impressive honor presented to him. One of the nation's leading universities was building a business program and a beautiful building, both named after Dr. Deming as a tribute to his remarkable contributions to American business. It was well done and appropriate, but Dr. Deming's response was surprising.

He simply said, "Thank you. Now turn to page 24 of your workbook." Everyone was puzzled but went right back to work. Was this humility, ungratefulness, or what? I found out when he signed my book. The first transformation I experienced, the Foams Plant (which I mentioned earlier), was well into its first year and was getting wonderful results. I related this to Dr. Deming, and added that I wanted to thank him for all he had done to make everyone's work life so much better in our facility.

That is when I heard the kind of response everyone expected when he received that wonderful honor just hours before. I can't remember all of his words because I was so surprised, but in essence what he said was this: "It's so gratifying for me to hear this report. This is *exactly* why I do what I do. It's so important to me that these transformations are successful and that people feel respected and productive in the workplace. I can't tell you how much it means to me for you to tell me of this experience." I think it's very clear that Dr. Deming was working for the people, not for himself. He couldn't have cared less for personal recognition, but show him an organization that was successful because of his contributions, and he was thrilled.

Dr. Deming's 14 Points follow. ***Those that are bold and italicized tie directly to the People Connection.*** As you can see, ten of them tie directly, and the remaining four are related, but indirectly. My comments are in parentheses following each point. Here are the Points[11]:

Origin of the 14 points:

"The 14 points apply anywhere, to small organizations as well as to large ones, to the service industry as well as to manufacturing. They apply to a division within a company."

The 14 points:

1. ***"Create constancy of purpose toward improvement of product and service, with the aim to become competitive and to stay in business, and to provide jobs."***
   (You must persevere, persevere, and persevere some more.)
2. ***"Adopt the new philosophy. We are in a new economic age. Western management must awaken to the challenge, must learn their responsibilities, and take on leadership for change."***
   (The old style leadership which worked quite well in years past no longer works, because the intensity of competition and expectations are much higher today.)
3. ***"Cease dependence on inspection to achieve quality. Eliminate the need for inspection on a mass basis by building quality into the product in the first place."***
   (If the process doesn't produce defect-free product or services, then it needs to be improved. The people who work in the process need

to be the ones to improve it. They need to be the ones to inspect the products or services as they are being produced. Scott's agency reduced its customer complaints by 99 percent in less than 6 months, not by quality control, but by improving the processes that produce *happy* customers.)

4. "End the practice of awarding business on the basis of price tag. Instead, minimize total cost. Move toward a single supplier for any one item, on a long-term relationship of loyalty and trust." (This point is not italicized because it does not *directly* relate to the People Connection. It does relate indirectly, however.)

   (The Decatur facility, probably like thousands of similar plants around the country, suffered from lack of service and quality that was caused by shopping for the lowest component price. When suppliers are forced to come up with the lowest price in a competitive environment where one penny can make all the difference, then they will cut corners in service and quality. For example, we had to improve supplier performance so the Decatur outsourcing project could be successful. When we collaborated with suppliers to improve service, we experienced some very surprising results. We ended up with much fewer suppliers, lead-times that were reduced by about 90 percent, and *another half million dollars in savings!* The benefits of collaboration are far greater than pitting suppliers against one another in price competition.)

5. *"Improve constantly and forever the system of production and service, to improve quality and productivity, and thus constantly decrease costs."*

   (The vision needs to be so challenging that it takes the team or organization on a never-ending journey of improvement.)

6. "Institute training on the job."

(People want to be great and to be a part of something great. Training is an excellent way to make that possible, and it is the one thing that employees request the most.)

7. *"Institute leadership. The aim of supervision should be to help people and machines and gadgets to do a better job. Supervision of management is in need of overhaul, as well as supervision of production workers."*

    (The role of leadership needs to change from command and control to a style of influence and participation.)

8. *"Drive out fear, so that everyone may work effectively for the company."*

    (The People Connection shows how to make it safe for open and honest communications – which is the same as driving out fear).

9. *"Break down barriers between departments. People in research, design, sales, and production must work as a team, to foresee problems of production and in use that may be encountered with the product or service."*

    (Everyone in the organization has a piece to the puzzle, and all the pieces need to be working in unison or the organization will not progress.)

10. *"Eliminate slogans, exhortations, and targets for the work force asking for zero defects and new levels of productivity. Such exhortations only create adversarial relationships, as the bulk of the causes of low quality and low productivity belong to the system and thus lie beyond the power of the work force.*

- *Eliminate work standards (quotas) on the factory floor. Substitute leadership.*

    - *Eliminate management by objective. Eliminate management by numbers, numerical goals. Substitute leadership."*

(Slogans, exhortations, and targets are, to a great extent, insulting to the workforce. Instead of management seeing its workforce as thinking and intelligent people doing the best they can with the current processes, exhortations tell the workforce that management sees them as needing to be told what to do.)

11. *"Remove barriers that rob the hourly worker of his right to pride of workmanship. The responsibility of supervisors must be changed from sheer numbers to quality."*

    (People who are removed from all of the intimate details of getting the job done frequently make the mistake of building processes that ignore many of these details. Empowering the workers to fix these processes substantially improves team performance.)

12. "Remove barriers that rob people in management and in engineering of their right to pride of workmanship. This means, *inter alia {among other things}*, abolishment of the annual or merit rating and of management by objective."

    (This point relates to the People Connection indirectly rather than directly. It's difficult to rate individual performance without hurting team performance. Team members who focus on ways to improve their individual rating will not always give their full attention to team efforts. Though team and individual performance is not always mutually exclusive, there's usually enough conflict to hurt the team. Unfortunately, the damage due to this conflict is difficult to identify and assess.)

13. Institute a vigorous program of education and self-improvement.

    (This point also relates indirectly. The People Connection unlocks the natural motivation and desire for education and self-improvement.)

14. *"Put everybody in the company to work to accomplish the trans-*
     formation. The transformation is everybody's job."

     (The People Connection is designed for full engagement so that all
     team members are involved in achieving the goal.)

     As you can see, there's a high level of agreement between
     Dr. Deming's 14 points and the People Connection, with no points
     of disagreement. This correlation helps validate the People Con-
     nection.

THE POLYETHYLENE PLANT

The second team in my journey of 10 different organizations that succeeded with the People Connection was the Polyethylene Plant, the sister
plant to the Foams Plant. This plant had started the SPI (Statistical Process
Improvement) program at the same time as the Foams Plant, but had much
the same experience as the other 18 plants in the company. They were not
able to achieve the results that Foams was. They did not connect with the
people like the Foams Plant did; and they also pursued specialized and very
sophisticated improvement programs like many of the other plants did.
They, like the others, grew to accept, in a year or two, that their program
was not meeting expectations.

> *The most successful American businesses today are the ones that fol-*
> *low Dr. Deming's 14 Points.*

My boss, Keith Baker, was assigned as plant manager of the Polyethylene Plant. He called on me to join him there as Quality Manager, so we
could create the same kind of changes that Foams experienced. The Polyethylene Plant was in much worse shape from a competitive standpoint
than the Foams Plant. The competition was fierce. The profit picture
– and our future – were grim. The situation was urgent.

One of the first lessons I learned there was how resilient and forgiving workforces are. No matter how many times management fails, the workforce will continue to remain receptive to a turn-around. We came back with the same message of change, reconnected solidly with all of our associates, and almost immediately found ourselves in an enthusiastic race for the goal.

Team skills training was a new program developed and introduced by corporate at this time. This was a three-day program designed to help people understand how to best work together as a team. We decided to provide this training after the teams had spent about three months working together. This delay increased trainee receptivity, because they could better relate to the topic – and they knew which questions to ask. This training was an invaluable addition to our efforts.

We were also asked to compete on a polyethylene products contract for Armstrong, the ceiling tile manufacturer. They were a Malcolm Baldrige Award finalist and were therefore intensely interested in quality. The Malcolm Baldrige Award is a difficult award to win, and it only goes to those companies who have truly mastered quality and the improvement process. We had to submit a 30-page questionnaire and tons of documentation regarding our quality program and improvement processes. An Armstrong delegation also spent two days on site, touring and interviewing us to better understand our program. At the end of this process they were very complimentary and gave us the highest marks. They also encouraged us to apply for ISO 9000 certification (International Organization for Standardization) since our program was already about 95 percent there. We had no need for, nor intentions of becoming ISO certified, which is normally regarded as an immense task, but we were pleasantly surprised at how close we were to it.

The Polyethylene Plant was rated a 9 on a 1-10 scale and the other Polyethylene facilities a 3 by Central Engineers, Business Managers, and Dave from corporate quality. We had surveyed about a dozen different individuals at different times and found the correlation between scores was within a point or two in each case. We then went to outside people such as sales people and consultants, and got basically the same scores, again within a point or two of the others. We clearly had arrived. The other plants continued to focus on enabling just a few of their star hourly associates, or on time-consuming problem-solving methodologies. Unfortunately, we still hadn't come to the full realization of what we had acquired so we did not push our solution vigorously enough to influence the other facilities.

Though the differences in our facility were readily apparent to many, no company managers seemed to be curious about what created those differences. This lack of interest is a common problem in command and control companies. Everybody has their eye on the boss, and not on what is going on around them. Plant Manager Peggy Sinclair noticed this same phenomenon in Ken Blanchard and Sheldon Bowle's book Gung Ho, Peggy Sinclair could not understand how Andy Longclaw's department in this true story could perform extraordinarily well without any other manager expressing even the slightest interest in how he was making it happen[12].

We were on a roll in the Polyethylene Plant, but the winds of change were reaching gale force. The Polyethylene Plant was only one of two plants that had succeeded with SPI and that was not enough to save the entire division. Our company, therefore, began making preparations to sell the division, so they could concentrate on their mainstream business. Huge downsizings were underway as the company trimmed us up for sale and looked for ways to improve short-term profitability. The Quality Program, and hence the SPI program, was the first to be eliminated. I decided to take the voluntary separation package and move on to a company where I could continue doing what I was doing. By this time, the People Connection was firmly entrenched in my blood.

THE FLYWHEEL

Perseverance, as we have seen, is crucial for implementing lasting and effective cultural change. We have seen it explained in the People Connection, and as the number one point in Dr. Deming's 14 Points. We have yet another validation of its importance in Jim Collin's <u>Good to Great.</u> Collins and his team thoroughly researched the factors that transitioned good companies into great companies. Only eleven companies out of the Fortune 500 qualified as those that transitioned from good-to-great, because the criteria were so strict. The basic pattern that each great company followed was: "fifteen-year cumulative stock returns at or below the general stock market, punctuated by a transition point, then cumulative returns at least three times the market for the next fifteen years."[13]

One of the common factors his team found in the great companies was what they called the "flywheel effect".

The best way to describe this flywheel effect is to quote Jim Collins: "Picture a huge, heavy flywheel – a massive metal disk mounted horizontally on an axle, about 30 feet in diameter, 2 feet thick, and weighing about 5,000 pounds. Now, imagine your task is to get the flywheel rotating on the axle as fast and long as possible. Pushing with great effort, you get the flywheel to inch forward, moving almost imperceptibly at first. You keep pushing and, after two or three hours of persistent effort, you get the flywheel to complete the entire turn."

In the People Connection progress also seems glacially slow. But that effort is going somewhere. It's building momentum with the people; eventually, their contributions make a difference; and you will notice what Collins' team noticed next.

"You're pushing no harder than during the first rotation, but the flywheel goes faster and faster. Each turn of the flywheel builds upon work done earlier, compounding your investment of effort. A thousand times faster, then ten thousand, then a hundred thousand. The huge disk flies forward, with almost unstoppable momentum."

What Jim Collins and his team discovered by studying these great companies is what we have seen each time using the People Connection. Now, Collins' most important point:

"The flywheel image captures the overall feel of what it was like inside the companies as they went from good to great. *No matter how dramatic the end result, the good-to-great transformations never happened in one fell swoop. There was no single defining action, no grand program, no one killer innovation, no solitary lucky break, no wrenching revolution. Good to great comes about by a cumulative process – step by step, action by action, decision by decision, turn by turn of the flywheel – that adds up to sustained and spectacular results.*"[14] (Italics mine).

> *"If you don't like the way the world is, you change it. You have an obligation to change it. You just do it one step at a time." Marian Wright Edelman , Founder of the "Leave No Child Behind" program.*

By employing the People Connection, I believe the flywheel will spin up much faster than what actually was experienced by the good-to-great companies. As I explained earlier, 20 to 30 percent improvements in the first three to six months are normal. As Figures 7A and 7B show, an organization can eliminate 95 percent of its service delays within just two years by following the efficient and effective People Connection. Here are some other interesting observations from Jim Collins:

"The good-to-great companies had no name for their transformations. There was no launch event, no tag line, no programmatic feel whatsoever."[15] *Remember Deming's tenth point, which was to eliminate slogans and exhortations from the workplace[16]. The name "People Connection" is used in this book to describe the Process, but I hope only the mindset and the meeting are remembered, not the name. Names are for programs, and this is not a program.*

"The good-to-great companies were subject to the same short-term pressures from Wall Street as the comparison companies. Yet, unlike the comparison companies, they had the patience and discipline to follow the buildup-breakthrough flywheel model despite these pressures."[17] *Patience is probably one of the hardest things about the People Connection, but it is also one of the keys to success.*

Now, here is another point by Jim Collins that has a strong similarity to the People Connection: "Clearly, the good-to-great companies did get incredible commitment and alignment – they artfully managed change – but they never really spent much time thinking about it."[18] I believe the "artful management of change" is a key part of the People Connection. Just the visioning process, alone, in the People Connection greatly accelerates commitment, alignment, and motivation.

I find this empirical evidence in 11 great companies very encouraging. It validates what we discovered by accident in the Foams Plant and what I have seen work nine times since. More than encouraging, it's exciting, because it says *the potential for greatness is in each one of our teams, if we do the right things and persevere.*

WHAT ELSE IS HAPPENING WHILE WE'RE PERSEVERING?

There are other things going on "below the waterline" also. The leader's perseverance provides people time to build trust in management. Trust, which is oftentimes interpreted as something ethical, is actually a bit different here. This trust means that the work force or team knows what to expect every day. They know they won't be subjected to flavors of the month. They will grow to believe that management is strong enough to stay the course. Teams tend to be amazingly forgiving once they sense they are on the right track.

Team members also have the time to build their understanding and skills and accomplish the work that is required to meet the goal they really want as much as management. Team members usually aren't as vocal about their commitments and plans as leaders would like them to be. It's hard, therefore, to know where they really are. If we use the People Connection and carefully watch all the signs, we will usually see a lot more going on than what meets the eye.

WHERE PERSEVERANCE LEADS YOU.

Finding the right way to get the job done; taking the time and effort required to correct and align the thinking; and then showing the fortitude to stay the course – in spite of all the distractions – truly does inspire a team. When the organization is inspired and is allowed to be great, then the customers win, the employees win, and the stockholders win. What's even better is that these wins are perfectly obvious to all observers, inside and outside. ***Everybody wins. This is the most exciting result of all. What more could we ask?***

∞ CHAPTER 16: BRINGING IT ALL TOGETHER

"We trained hard...but it seemed that every time we were beginning to form up into teams, we would be reorganized. I was to learn later in life that we tend to meet any new situation by reorganizing; and a wonderful method it can be for creating the illusion of progress while producing confusion, inefficiency and demoralization."
– Gaius Petronius, Arbiter 60 A.D./Rome

THE NEEDS OF THE ORGANIZATION

America will not be able to keep up with the rest of the world if we don't change the way we think. People in many countries are willing to work for less than two dollars per hour, and profit-squeezed companies can't resist following the crowd that is already outsourcing. The world has plenty of work to be done. We have more than enough need for workers in America, but **_not_** if we view them as financial burdens. Employees are investments, not burdens. They are also the reason for existence of our companies. Our attitudes about employees are creating unhappy workers in record numbers and a crisis for our country.

The People Connection offers a simple prescription on how to unleash employees to create amazing results. These results will excite the workers, the customers, the bosses, and the stockholders. This prescription is far more effective in global competition than any other. The People Connection is very simply:

∞ Thinking differently about people and teams.

∞ Establishing and maintaining an exciting vision.

∞ Letting the team determine and implement the plans to achieve the vision.

So much of the amazing power in the People Connection comes from people wanting to be great and to be a part of something great. Just look at the success of Rick Warren's book <u>The Purpose Driven Life.</u> In just a few short years, it has broken all the best selling book records at more than 25 million copies sold. People are starving for a purpose and want their work to be a fulfillment of that purpose.

It's very easy to miss the subtle things that make all the difference. I believe one of the subtle things that hurts us is our American culture, which is enamored with the quick and dramatic fixes, and shuns those that are difficult – especially those that involve working with people. Managers are typically attracted by numbers and data and shy away from people (the soft stuff). It helps to remember Tom Malone's quote: "It's the soft stuff that is the hard stuff, but it's the soft stuff that makes the difference."

It's also important to remember that one of Japan's leaders in organizational success, Masaaki Imai, says that, "Workers must be inspired to fulfill their roles, to feel proud of their jobs, and to appreciate the contribution they make to their company and society. Instilling a sense of mission and pride is an integral part of management's responsibility."[19] These feelings cannot be instilled by telling the team what to think through speeches, slogans, and newsletters. The only way is to win them over by offering them ownership in the process. Let's not be too critical of Western culture. After all, Henry Ford, Dr. Deming, Peter Drucker and Tom Paterson are the fathers of today's world-class organizational thinking, and *all are Americans*.

With the People Connection, the leader no longer sees the team as a group of individuals who need development and coordination. The leader will now see them all as one team, with a distinct team personality that needs nurturing, guidance, and challenges, just like an individual would.

The leader's job actually becomes easier, for they are now leading one team, instead of many individuals.

THE RESPONSE OF THE TEAM

The team, itself, will develop more rules and tougher rules. These rules will be much better designed and far less resisted, because they are designed for a purpose in which the team deeply believes. As Tom Peters, a leading expert on organizational improvement and author of several books, pointed out, high performing teams are highly disciplined. Team members expect more of one another – and receive it – than do leaders in traditional environments.

Team members will enjoy their work much more with the People Connection. They'll be more excited on the job. Most of them will look forward to getting to work. Team members will begin challenging their leaders, and not because the leaders aren't leading. The team is beginning to think on its own, develop its own ideas, and ask more questions than ever before.

Team leaders will have reservations about the decisions the teams are making. As long as the process is being followed and as long as their decisions do not risk someone's safety or break the law, there's no need to worry. If there is disagreement on a decision, then it's more than likely that all relevant information was not adequately communicated. It is therefore important to trust team decisions to the ones that have the most relevant information.

THE POWER OF THE VISION

In addition to the power of the team's need to be great, is the power that comes from a common vision. Developing a deeply held, exciting and effective vision that has total team buy-in requires a lot of time, effort, and reflection. Elaborate vision statement efforts are a waste of time. *A vision statement that cannot be instantly and enthusiastically recited by each team member adds no power to a team.*

The most effective way to communicate the vision is to take 5 minutes of meeting time every week for two to three months to discuss it. It needs to be a two-way dialogue. Far too many managers ignore this subtle, but critical, need because it seems "to be overkill". It's also necessary for a leader to have a significant amount of one-on-one dialogues with individual team members about the vision.

The team leader must ensure that the proper environment has been created for this fragile vision development process, particularly during the weekly meeting. *It's important that the team leader neither praise, nor criticize, input from individuals.* The team leader should then fold all of their comments into a wrap-up at the end of the short vision session, in order to show the progress of the consensus and to recognize <u>*all*</u> these inputs as important and valuable.

The real power of the vision comes from aligning the hundreds and thousands of decisions that the typical team makes in a day. These decisions easily escape the notice of the casual observer, but have a huge collective impact. *The quality of decisions isn't nearly as important as their timeliness and who owns them.* In other words, high quality decisions that come too late or don't fit the team's needs are not as good as lower quality decisions that do fit.

A vision statement that cannot be instantly and enthusiastically recited by each team member adds no power to a team.

Teams that cannot work together almost invariably do not share the same vision. Once the vision misconnects have been resolved, then the team can be brought back quickly to cooperative action.

Once the vision is firmly established, resistance to change rapidly melts away. Human beings are actually wired for change. Unfortunately, change is often associated with bad experiences in poorly managed change processes. People welcome change that gets them closer to the vision they have bought into.

NURTURING THE TEAM

The journey to the vision needs to be monitored and measured. People need to see progress, in other words "to see the chips fly". The measurement needs to be directly tied to the goal and needs to be as simple as possible. A single measurement is ideal.

By routinely reviewing these measurements, a number of things will happen to drive the team much closer to the vision:

- ∞ Visibility – Everybody sees what is happening and what is causing it.
- ∞ Priority setting – They know what is important because of the time and effort being spent on it.
- ∞ Influence decisions – Visibility and priority will influence the many "invisible" decisions they make outside the meeting.
- ∞ Buy-in – The discussion and action items will increase understanding, acceptance, ownership, excitement, and commitment to the goal.

"Buy-in" is acceptance and understanding, not a vote. Voting is different and is a great tool for selecting from a number of alternatives. Buy-in needs careful nurturing by the leader. The team needs the time to process new ideas, directives, and situations by discussing them, questioning them, challenging them, getting them wrong and learning from their mistakes. Most people, and especially the "team personality", learn and buy in best by doing these things and then leaving their imprint on it. To ensure this happens most effectively, *the team leader, in particular, must be vigilant about ensuring that each team member has been heard and understood by the rest of the team.*

Careful attention to the visioning process, the buy-in process, and all the little decisions required to achieve the goal seems to take a lot of time. In spite of this, the People Connection is actually faster than any other process in developing significant and sustainable gains. To prevent the negative consequences of being overwhelmed by impatience, it's important to keep meeting minutes and notes about the team's progress and refer to them when such distress strikes.

These written records are also great for celebrations. Celebrations that include the time to remember the journey with all its trials and tribulations are far richer than those that only celebrate victories. Less than five percent of our work is victory, the remaining 95 percent is the hard work and trial and error required to achieve it. Teams really enjoy reliving the feelings, the hard work, the key learnings, and their experiences with their teammates.

PREPARING THE LEADER

Different things will be required of a leader in this process. The leader can no longer be the boss, or the "king of the hill". The leader must see their team as number one – not the customer, and not their career. Their *team* must see the customer as number one. Every team member will have the opportunity to take a leadership role. Though a team needs only one leader driving the vision, it needs many leaders showing the way to get to the goal.

The People Connection will feel uncomfortable to most leaders until they understand and accept the new paradigm. Once understood, it will feel natural and comfortable. Sally Ride, our first female U.S. astronaut, had this to say: "All adventures, especially into new territory, are scary."

The leader and the team members need to understand and act on four simple principles. These are:

1. *People want to be great and to be a part of something great.*

2. *Most team activities involve a lot of waste due to variation, and the team needs to remove this waste by using basic Six Sigma principles. Six Sigma is the removal of variation in the process, because variation is the root of quality problems, customer dissatisfaction, and a lot of waste.*

3. *Most team activities also involve a lot of waste due to wasted time, effort, and money, and the team needs to remove this waste by using basic Lean principles. Lean is single-piece flow and the removal of waste from any process.*

4. *People need to trust and rely on one another to cover their blind spots which will allow them to see the complete picture.*

Everyone has blind spots, including the best of leaders. Many demands are placed on leadership, and courage is one of the foremost. It takes courage to rely on others to fill in our blind spots. Leaders should not be lured into false confidence by compliments, displayed respect, and affirming words. *No leader can, by their perceptions alone, lead a great team.*

A team can be no better than the quality of the leader's thinking. What a leader thinks about people, the problems facing the team, and improvement programs has a profound impact on a team's performance. Unfortunately, management usually falls into the trap of believing that poor team members and problems beyond their control are the primary reasons for poor performance. These are the leaders who will look to the next improvement program to fix what they themselves should be fixing. *Fixing their mindset should be their first priority.*

The 60 percent in the middle have the most to offer a team. The 20 percent on the top are doing the best they can and really can't do much more. The 20 percent on the bottom can't, or won't, perform. The 60 percent in the middle outnumber the other two put together by 50 percent. They're also far more responsive to leadership, whether it's good or bad.

A leader should also remember that it's never clear who exactly is in each of these three groups. There's no need to know because people are regularly moving from group to group, and because the 20 percent on the bottom will eventually disappear as a result of the process.

Leaders need to understand that teams can abuse this stratification of work performance by setting up a "pecking order" which is unhealthy. The leader needs to neutralize this tendency by spending a few minutes a meeting (for at least a few meetings) to ensure that the team understands a key principle. This principle is best illustrated with the puzzle analogy, which shows that it's impossible to be a great team without a complete picture, and no piece is less important than another in completing this picture.

Once the puzzle analogy has been absorbed by the team, then another principle becomes important to share. This principle is called "resonance", and it's a measure of how well the team is working together. Evolving the puzzle analogy into an acoustic guitar analogy, we can better understand resonance. If each piece of the guitar is fitted snugly together, then plucking the strings will create beautiful music. The degree of this response is called "resonance". When we feel like we've had a very good day where everyone was working together smoothly and harmoniously, then we've had a day that was high in resonance. The place could have flooded, but if the team worked great together, then resonance is still high.

MONITORING TEAM PROGRESS

It's important that the team understand the concept of resonance and to track their progress in improving it. Resonance is best rated subjectively on a 1 to 10 Leikert scale once per week, or so. These ratings should be tracked by the leaders; and anytime a trend seems to be developing they need to follow up. Brief, outside-the-meeting discussions are the best place to inquire about any developing trends. A team should not expect to be at a nine or 10 for at least a year or two. Also, a team needs to be regularly reminded that resonance measures *the process*, and not the results.

As team resonance increases, the bottom 20 percent will slowly begin to disappear. Many of the "trouble-makers" who were simply trying to tell management something will become the strongest converts, and the misfits and incorrigibles will not be able to stand the pressure from them. Peer pressure, always more effective than "boss pressure", will make the bottom 20 uncomfortable enough to reform, or to leave.

The weekly meetings are the tip of the iceberg. The process that the leader models in these weekly meetings gets used the rest of the week. Much of this activity is invisible since it's so hard to notice, but the collective impact is huge. The Foams Plant had a 33 percent improvement in profits that was a total surprise to everyone, because no one expected all those little contributions to add up to so much.

Even though this Process really is fast, it requires much patience and perseverance. Dr. Deming said to "stay the course" and Jim Collins told us of the "flywheel effect". All of the good to great companies experienced the feeling of a slow transition. As Collins pointed out, "greatness comes about by a cumulative process."

The People Connection is not a program; it's a way of thinking and involving people. Dr. Deming said to eliminate slogans and exhortations from the workplace. I think programs should be eliminated also, at least until a strong People Connection is built.

One last word on patience comes from Jim Collins. The good-to-great companies were subject to the same short-term pressures from Wall Street as the comparison companies but they had the patience and discipline to do what was right despite these pressures.[20]

Integrity is difficult, also. Leaders need to show integrity in everything they do. Sometimes, all we can lead with is a "trust me". Patience and integrity also allow the team the time and environment to build trust in management. This trust means that the team knows what to expect every day – because they can depend on leadership to do the right thing.

High integrity helps promote open and honest communications, which is a crucial need for any team. The leader must set the example for integrity and communications, and can expect the team to follow. Open and honest communications are the most effective tools in achieving outstanding team performance.

∞ CHAPTER 17: IMPLEMENTATION

"The first step to leadership is servanthood."
– John Maxwell

The People Connection and its principles have been fully explained. Troy Brandt, the Decatur Plant's Engineering Manager once said this Process is "simply a mindset". That description is pretty much on target. However, there are a few things we need to remember that give structure to the Process, such as the meeting disciplines, the small handful of tools mentioned earlier, and the implementation steps.

The mindset consists of how we think about our team, its members, and our role on that team. The mindset is what we need to change first. It's the mindset that will ultimately drive all other improvements.

The following implementation plan is the one I always use. It works great in all situations, especially urgent ones. Because of its basic and very streamlined nature, I recommend that you skip none of the steps. Here they are:

STEP 1: PREPARE YOURSELF

Read and understand this book. Read it twice, if it doesn't resonate the first time. There's no extra charge for additional readings. Resolve your questions before proceeding if you are leading the effort. If you are a leader, then have a heart-to-heart talk with your ego. If this mindset repulses you, then this Process won't work. Don't even think about faking it. If you are simply uncomfortable, but really want to make it work, then the team will support you. They will support the one who is sincerely trying, and will quietly and politely withhold support from the faker. Almost everyone who reads this book can lead a team using these principles, so don't let cold feet stop you. Though your new leadership role may seem foreign and disconcerting at first, you will ultimately adjust to it. One leader said it made him feel "discombobulated" at first. Today he is thrilled. *All you have to do is believe it, do it, and the good feelings will come later.*

This process is not a "believe it when you see it" kind of thing. <u>*As a leader, you must believe it first to see it.*</u> Team members usually find it easy to believe. In 22 years of experience, I've discovered that it's the managers who have the hardest time transitioning to this process. Many of them can't even see it. They have to overcome ego, as well as sacrifice a way of life they think has been good to them. They are on top of their mountain, and they worked and fought hard to get there. Managers and leaders who are not willing to give this up are seriously short-changing themselves and their teams. They're missing out on an even better mountain if they can't find a way to modify their ego.

Your team wants to be great, even that quiet little old grandmother. She wants the team to win, just like everyone else, and she will work just as hard. She may appear to be gentle as a lamb, but hidden away she has the heart of a tiger. Why not let her and the rest of the team drive for greatness? They can make *your* ride better than you ever could by yourself – no matter how talented and hard-working you are. A key part of a leader's role is humility. Your team will see you as humble, if you freely admit you are learning and will make many mistakes. You also need to listen carefully and learn from them. This humility is one of your greatest assets, because teams perform best for humble and effective leaders. You provide the humility and the effectiveness will come from following the Process.

STEP 2: PREPARE THE TEAM

As a leader, you will need to spend some one-on-one time with each of your team members. If the team is too big, then talk with a representative sample. Plan to talk to at least 15 to 20 people. Twenty to 30 minutes with each one is sufficient time for you to understand what it is they see and need. Mostly, just ask questions and listen. I do *not* recommend using formal surveys or taking notes. Both of these will bias and hamper the feedback. *This process stresses connection, not administration; listening and understanding, not documentation.* They need to feel totally safe in giving you open and honest input. Taking notes creates fear in the back of their minds that what they are saying can come back to haunt them. Surveys will also constrain the feedback to a preconceived format. You need free-form feedback. Then you can pursue immediately those unexpected and, oftentimes, subtle comments that can lead you to some great insights. It's important to communicate that the intent of the People Connection is to make the team more effective, not to solve problems. End by assuring team members again, that what they say will be held in confidence.

Take some time to reflect on this feedback. Accept your team's view, and don't twist it to make it conform to yours. *The old expression "perception is reality" is still true, so don't underestimate its pit bull tenacity.* Perception will expose problems you wouldn't normally be able to see. Solving these problems is usually less important than being aware of them.

The information your team provides will also help you decide on a vision that best fits the needs of the company, your team, the individual team members, and the customer. For example, Scott's team members felt that they weren't pleasing the customer and that trying to win the trophy would just aggravate the situation. However, an agency needs to sell policies to stay in business. What finally resonated with the team is when they finally saw the trophy as a measure of how many happy customers they had. This goal fit the needs of the business, the customers, *and* its team members. Everybody wins with a carefully selected and communicated vision.

You should almost never replace team members. In all 10 of the transformations I have worked with, not a single person was replaced in order to make the transformation successful. It's almost impossible to predict who will, and who won't, make it in the People Connection. People who I never thought would make it became top performers. Most of those who couldn't make it, left on their own. I believe replacing team members in advance of a transformation is a waste of time; potentially a waste of good people; plus, it runs a high risk of sending the wrong messages to the remaining team members. Firing or replacing people puts everyone else on edge, and throws up defensive barriers of all kinds, as well as reduces confidence in the People Connection. It's simply not worth it.

After this relatively short preparation time, the team is now ready to go. The leader has taken the time to prepare his or her mindset. The team members have provided their input, and the leader has listened. Just about everything else can be done on the fly from here on out. *It takes only a little talk, but a lot of action to make the People Connection successful.*

The only other preparation that might help is for the team to meet for a few hours before their first regular meeting, in order to get a more thorough understanding of what to expect. This will reduce some of the uncertainties, concerns, and confusion that could surface later. This can also be done by installments during the regular all-staff meetings, but it will take weeks longer.

Step 3: Conduct your weekly meetings

The People Connection specifies a one-hour meeting once per week. The first five minutes of this meeting involves a clarification of the vision. The next 50 minutes asks what it will take to get there, and involves everyone possible in implementing the ideas. The last 5 minutes are for plus/deltas and resonance. The plus/deltas answer the question "what are we doing well and what can we do better?" Resonance addresses how well the team is working together. ***The team needs to understand that how they are working together (process) is just as important as the results (content).*** High performing teams keep an equal balance of process and content. Content is the focus for the middle 50 minutes of the meeting and process is the focus for the last five minutes of the meeting. The meeting needs to end promptly to maintain good meeting discipline, and to set the example for all other meetings.

You might think that if the process is all that important, then why shouldn't there be more than five minutes spent on it? That's an excellent question and there's an excellent answer. The fact is that this five minute time slot is simply a meeting of all the minds. It gets everyone synchronized every week. The process gets a lot of attention from leaders and team members outside the meeting. The balance of the process, and the content, is carefully maintained by simply following the People Connection.

The leader needs to regularly clarify that the last five minutes of the meeting relate strictly to the process. If the results (content) were bad all week, but the team was in top form the entire time, then they should get very high resonance scores. On the other hand, if the results were great, but the team wasn't clicking, then they should get low resonance scores. If the team sees an opportunity to improve results by improving their process, then that should be noted as a delta, or what they can do better. The process must be good before the results can be. Good results without a good process is simply luck that will soon run out. If the team is doing something that is producing good results, then they should note that as a plus. Lots of pluses are important, because a team usually gets more of what it focuses on.

The team leader needs to remember the remarkable power in the question "what will it take to get there?" *Do not assign* people to work on an opportunity that answers this question. That gets back to the old "command and control" style of leadership. When opportunities are identified by the team, *ask for volunteers to address them.* If team leaders themselves see an opportunity, then they should ask the right questions to get the team to see it. If they can, fine. If they can't, then they should drop it, and wait for an opportunity to try again later.

> *It takes only a little talk, but a lot of action to make the People Connection successful.*

If the team is overwhelmed by too many opportunity choices, then the leader should ask which one will get the team closest to the vision? If the opportunities are equal, then there is more than one right answer, so the team should pick the one they like the most.

This Process has worked very well in 500-person facilities and it has worked very well in 20-person organizations. Scalability is not a concern. The Process is also flexible enough to work with whatever your organizational structures and strategic and tactical plans are. It is not necessary to make organizational or strategic plan changes in advance, nor is it advisable. These changes can best be made later using the insights gained from the People Connection.

It's essential for the leader of an organization or facility to take an active role in the People Connection. Large facilities and companies, of course, present problems of time and coordination that they're already dealing with. The People Connection doesn't add to these challenges, because it quickly relieves a lot of the existing problems. Having the facility leader, head coach, or CEO visibly involved and supportive, will help ensure unity.

Larger organizations also present problems with group size. I recommend no more than 20 per group for the weekly working meetings. All groups should meet together on some kind of regular basis such as monthly or quarterly, simply for sharing information such as team performance and progress. Everyone needs to be involved in both the small working group meetings and the large group meetings. The facility leader should lead the informational meetings, just as the team leader leads the working group meetings.

STEP 4: CONTINUOUSLY MONITOR THE PROCESS AND RESULTS

Everyone on the team needs to monitor the results (content). Everyone also needs to monitor the process (how the team is working together), especially the team leader. Regularly checking with team members outside the meeting will reveal important things about the process that won't necessarily come up in the weekly meetings.

Results need to be displayed as simple graphs, if at all possible. The graphs show which way the score is going. The People Connection drives evolutionary change, not revolutionary change. Historical data in graphical format, therefore, is necessary to track progress. Graphs such as those on page 61 meet these requirements, because they track progress. Six Sigma provides even more sophisticated graphs (e.g. run and control charts) for monitoring results. I recommend these graphs be considered for your activities.

I cannot overstress the importance of monitoring results – including those of individual team members. Each team and team member needs to be able to demonstrate to themselves and to others daily that they are doing what they need to do to reach the goal. A high performing team needs to know where they're going (the vision), how to work together (the People Connection), and to have each team member do their part (individual performance). These three areas are mutually supportive. When one improves or needs to improve, so do the others.

I have developed an allergic reaction to administrative and program tools, because I have observed for many years that they become the goal, instead of a means to the end. That's one reason there are so few tools in this book. *I want to stress that the mindset and the process rule, not the tools. Many tools can work wonders, but only if the mindset and process are working well first.* However, I did make several exceptions. These exceptions are the team assessment tool on page 9, the graphs I just mentioned, and the sustaining checklist on page 182.

The sustaining checklist is essential. This tool should be used jointly by the team leaders and their process partner(s) to ensure that all items are checked on a weekly basis. It's not critical to ensure there's a checkmark in each cell every week; but it's critical to ensure that no unhealthy trends occur. By the end of this 21-week cycle, the habits should be established well enough that the checklist can be discontinued. If the habits aren't firmly entrenched, then the checklist should be continued until it is.

> *The mindset and the process rule, not the tools. Many tools can work wonders, but only if the mindset and process are working well first.*

Remember, your progress with the People Connection will appear irregular. It will move forward at a rapid rate for a period of time, and then seem to regress, or falter. It's a lot like working our way through a mountain range. When we're at the top of the first mountain, the view is thrilling and fulfilling. Time rolls on and drives us off the top. We can't go back and we can't go any higher until we pass through the valley on the other side of the mountain. This valley is not so much a time of regression as it is the developmental process that enables the team to climb the next mountain – which should be even higher. The priority, therefore, should be directed at properly navigating the valley in order to arrive at the right mountain.

> *There will be mountain tops and valleys throughout this journey; but the successful journey is the one that leads to successively higher peaks, not the one that avoids the valleys. There is no avoiding the valleys.*

STEP 5: GET OUTSIDE HELP

The People Connection, as you've probably noticed, is internally focused. It's focused on team development that will contribute heavily to a team's competitiveness and survival. However, competitiveness can be significantly improved by going beyond the People Connection. This book focuses on the People Connection because most teams need it badly. Going beyond the People Connection is usually easy for most teams.

Dr. Deming frequently asserted that "all knowledge comes from the outside". If your team sees nothing beyond their own boundaries, then they are in grave danger of falling behind, or stuck on a dead-end street in this fast-changing world. There are endless opportunities to learn from others how the world is changing and how to do things better. There are seminars, trade magazines, conventions, training classes, new programs and consultants.

There is also a process called the "Tom Paterson Process", which I highly recommend. Tom Paterson was introduced in Chapter 13. This process is a seamless bolt-on to the People Connection. It adds two critical things to the People Connection, as well as many others less critical. The first thing it adds is a strategic plan, and the second is a formal method for renewing the organization. The philosophical alignment between the People Connection and the Tom Paterson Process is complete, which is what makes it such a seamless addition.

The Tom Paterson Process is essentially a strategic operations planning process that puts the entire strategic plan on one page. This is a remarkable improvement over the typical process that fills a thick notebook, which gathers dust on a shelf because no one has time to read it. The Tom Paterson Process is user friendly and lends itself to a quick start, easy and frequent follow-up and effective renewal. The strategic plan itself only takes three days of team time. The follow-up takes about an hour each week to an hour each month. The renewal process is attractive to most teams, because it uses the "idea bucket". This bucket insulates the team from the frequent disruption caused by new ideas, metering them out at the appropriate time and place where they can do the most good.

The Tom Paterson Process also contributes heavily to energizing a team. The team gains a deep understanding of the business, the vision, and which improvements are needed. The People Connection and the Tom Paterson Process together will lead your team to results you never dreamed possible.

Checklist for Sustaining a Team's Rate of Improvement

Week	1	2	3	4	5	6	7	8	9	10	11	12	13	14	15	16	17	18	19	20	21
Outside the Meeting																					
Ask 3 different team members how it is going																					
Before the Meeting																					
Plan and publish the purpose and agenda for the meeting																					
During the Meeting																					
Ensure the vision is crystal clear																					
Discuss the results																					
Ask "what will it take to get there?" at least once																					
Lead the middle 60 percent																					
Let the team lead as much of the discussion as possible																					
Drive their improvement action items as much as is practical																					
Address resonance and what it will take to improve it																					
After the Meeting																					
Debrief with process partner(s)																					
Determine the team's needs																					
Plan and implement actions to meet the team's needs																					
Document minutes and team status																					

Figure 17A: Checklist for sustaining a team's rate of improvement

∞ CHAPTER 18: WE HAVE REACHED THE SUMMIT!

"Leadership is not magnetic personality – that can just as well be a glib tongue. It is not "making friends and influencing people" – that is flattery. Leadership is lifting a person's vision to high sights, the raising of a person's performance to a higher standard, the building of a personality beyond normal limitations."
– Peter F. Drucker

THE NEW LEADERSHIP DISCIPLINE

People Connection leaders think and behave differently. They no longer give orders. They see their team – not the customer – as number one. Leaders will no longer be "king of the mountain" with everyone looking up to them, but instead share a higher mountain with the entire team. Leaders establish and sustain the vision; ensure the teams are properly supported; and then trust the teams to make and implement the decisions to reach the vision.

Leaders will see that their organizations exist for the employees, with customers and stockholders as beneficiaries. The key to success and *the reason for that success* is the team. Without them, there can be no happy customers or stockholders. They are part of the organization because they need an income, and perhaps more importantly, they need purpose, meaning and fulfillment.

Leaders understand these needs. They understand the visioning process and the way to engage the team in reaching it. They understand how best to connect with their team members. Leaders keep this Process working with almost fanatical zeal. They lead the all-staff meetings and stay constantly out in front ensuring that the team stays on track.

They see integrity as critical. Many times during cultural change, integrity alone will carry the day. When leaders model integrity, the organization will follow. Much of the power of this Process comes from integrity and its close associate: unimpeded open and honest communications, another thing the People Connection stimulates.

Understanding your role…perfectly

The key to making team members successful is to create the right environment for them to succeed. No one has to create success for them; they want to do it themselves. They want to own their jobs and earn the meaning and fulfillment associated with those jobs. This will happen when leaders and team members follow the People Connection and throw everything they have into it.

Let's recall the comments the Conyers Plant staff made about "these people" (referring to the hourly people). "These people have no motivation; they have no education; and they have no ability to get our plant to the next level." I responded with: "The only differences between these people and those of us in this room are the decisions we made in life." I had no idea the actual proof of my statement was just around the corner.

When all of our hourly workers' old jobs were eliminated by the new contract, they were required to take verbal and math aptitude tests. These tests were to ensure they had the basic skills required to successfully complete the training for the new line-up of jobs as defined in the new contract. Jack Anderson, the VP of Manufacturing, wisely required all of the salaried people to take the same tests as the hourly.

It was so exciting to see that the profile of test scores for the hourly associates was basically the same as for the salaried workforce! Vindication was sweet, but sweeter still, we all saw, in objective terms, that there really was no difference between management and our team members. Team members were every bit as capable as those who were in the offices, with the exception of a small number of illiterates in the hourly profile.

__Now, here is a crucial point about what a leader's role should be:__

There has recently been an increasing level of interest in "servant-leadership". Though I believe servant-leadership is the best style of leadership, it's easily and widely misunderstood. The word "servant" can be distasteful to many, because it sounds like cleaning toilets for the team. It's also rejected by many, because it seems demeaning or unbefitting to those who have studied hard, worked hard, and clawed their way to the top. Clearly, little competition exists for the title "servant-leader".

Contrary to these unenthusiastic points of view, servant-leadership is the highest form of leadership. It carries the highest honors and highest rewards, though they are much less conspicuous, direct and personal. Servant-leadership is a mindset in which leaders see themselves as no better than any other team member. If cleaning toilets is part of our leadership role, then we need to do it – quietly. Those who do it to impress the team or outsiders are not servant-leaders, but rather self-serving leaders. And as the term implies, a servant-leader must *__lead__* as well as *__serve__* – courageously and unselfishly. That balance is crucial – and demanding.

Jim Collins, in his book <u>Good to Great</u>, tells us of his team's unexpected and remarkable discovery that the 11 companies to make the "Good to Great" list were all led by "Level 5" leaders[21]. "Level 5" leaders are, in essence, servant-leaders with huge ambitions for their teams, but not themselves. *__Every single one of these 11 companies was led by a servant-leader "on afterburners"__*. Level 5 leaders lead for the sake of the team, not for their own gain. They were all quiet, self-effacing CEO's, who hardly anyone ever hears about. It might help to keep in mind that these great companies all outperformed their closest competitors by at least three times in financial performance. By contrast, companies led by well-known celebrities didn't make the list of greats.

Jim Collins' team actually found that celebrity leaders quite surprisingly hurt their companies. It appears leaders can focus on making themselves look good or their teams look good, but cannot do both[22].

To give you a perspective on Jim Collins' "Level 5 Leadership", here are a few excerpts from his book. The first is the "Level 5 Hierarchy" which goes like this:

- ∞ "Level 5 – Level 5 Executive [capability, not position]: Builds enduring greatness through a paradoxical blend of personal humility and professional will."
- ∞ "Level 4 – Effective Leader: Catalyzes commitment to and vigorous pursuit of a clear and compelling vision, stimulating higher performance standards."
- ∞ " Level 3 – Competent Manager: Organizes people and resources toward the effective and efficient pursuit of predetermined objectives."
- ∞ "Level 2 – Contributing Team Member: Contributes individual capabilities to the achievement of group objectives and works effectively with others in a group setting."
- ∞ "Level 1 – Highly Capable Individual: Makes productive contributions through talent, knowledge, skills, and good work habits."

Collins continues, "Level 5 leaders are a study in duality: modest and willful, humble and fearless. It is very important to grasp that Level 5 leadership is not just about humility and modesty. It is equally about ferocious resolve, an almost stoic determination to do whatever needs to be done to make the company great. [The Level 5 leader] acts with quiet, calm determination; relies principally on inspired standards, not inspiring charisma, to motivate."[23]

Collins also provides his hypothesis about who is capable of Level 5 leadership. He believes there is a small group that will never be able to place their egoistic needs below the "greater ambition of building something larger and more lasting than themselves". The rest of the people have the "potential to evolve to Level 5; the capability resides within them, perhaps buried or ignored, but there nonetheless. And under the right circumstances – self-reflection, conscious personal development, a mentor, a great teacher, loving parents, a significant life experience, a Level 5 boss, or any number of other factors – they begin to develop."[24]

Jim Collins is saying that probably a large percentage of us have a shot at attaining Level 5 leadership. I believe that's true. It's ironic that those with the highest drive for personal recognition cannot outperform those whose ambition lies with the team rather than themselves.

How often has it been said that the more you give to others, the more you get in return? Collins' findings seems to give new weight to this old saying. Why would leaders, who want to be the best, be willing to settle for something that goes no further than their own selfish interests?

All we have to do is take the high road, and ensure that our *team* earns the recognition. Jim Collins stiffly resisted his team's discovery of Level 5 leadership, thinking that some other mechanism than leadership makes a company great[25]. But the data spoke so loudly that he and his team simply could not ignore it. As they so ably proved, *the greatest leaders in business today are servant-leaders.*

The parallels between Level 5 Leaders and People Connection leaders are unmistakable. People Connection leaders are focused on meeting the needs of the team, instead of their personal needs. People Connection leaders focus on a very simple vision that people will get excited about, which means that it must be an ambitious and audacious one. Similarly, Level 5 leaders were "incredibly ambitious" and set seemingly impossible goals for their teams.

The roots of servant-leadership go back at least 20 centuries when Jesus of Nazareth taught, "*whoever wants to become great among you must be*

your servant, and whoever wants to be first must be your slave..." This is
a concise definition of servant leadership.

In the <u>Servant Leader</u>, by Ken Blanchard and Phil Hodges, "When we
talk about servant leadership, most people think that means the "inmates
are running the prison", or the leader is trying to please everyone. People
who think this way don't understand that there are two parts of leadership
that Jesus exemplified: A visionary role – doing the right things; and an
implementation role – doing things right."

Another hard-hitting quote from the Servant Leader is: *"**<u>The ultimate
sign of an effective leader is what happens when you are not there. That
was the power of Jesus' leadership – the leaders He trained went on to
change the world when He was no longer with them in bodily form</u>.**"*[26]

To me, *servant-leadership is not boastful, it is serving. Servant-
leadership is not soft, it is powerful.*

There is an instructive proverb from antiquity about servant-leadership
that actually came out of a fortune cookie, though its veracity has been vali-
dated by similar quotes from that time. "The mark of a truly great leader
is when you can't pick him out from the rest of the team." I believe this
proverb says that great leaders create great teams, who create great results
by allowing the teams' achievements to blossom through the leadership
of each team member. When all team members are allowed to grow and
develop as leaders, then the difference between them and the leader is almost indistinguishable. As Jim Collins said – "There are Level 5 leaders all
around us", which is why every one of our teams has infinite potential.

LEADERSHIP QUOTES

"The Great Tao (leader) nurtures all things without lording it over anyone. It holds what it makes, yet never fights to do so: that is why we call it great. Why? Because it never tries to be so." Tao Te Ching.

"The sage's (leader's) way, Tao, is the way of water. The sage needs to know like water how to flow around the blocks and how to find the way through. Like water, the sage should wait for the moment to ripen and be right; water, you know, never fights; it flows around without harm." Tao Te Ching.

"Leadership is the capacity to translate vision into reality." Warren Bennis

"Leadership is practiced not so much in words as in attitude and in actions." Harold Geneen

"Leadership is influence." John Maxwell

"Leadership is an action, not a position." Donald H. McGannon

"You cannot be a leader, and ask other people to follow you, unless you know how to follow, too." Sam Rayburn

"The main characteristics of effective leadership are intelligence, integrity or loyalty, mystique, humor, discipline, courage, self sufficiency and confidence." James L. Fisher

"Be gentle and be bold; be frugal and you can be liberal; avoid putting yourself before others and you can become a leader among men." Lao Tzu

"To get others to come into our ways of thinking, we must go over to theirs; and it is necessary to follow, in order to lead." William Hazlitt

---

MORE LEADERSHIP QUOTES

"I have nothing to offer but blood, toil, tears, and sweat." Winston Churchill

"Leaders don't force people to follow them – they invite them on a journey." Charles S. Lauer

"A leader is best when people barely know he exists, not so good when people obey and acclaim him, worse when they despise him... But of a good leader who talks little when his work is done, his aim fulfilled, they will say, "We did it ourselves."" Lao Tzu

---

I hope this book has taught us how to think and act like servant-leaders on afterburners, regardless of our role on the team. Cleaning toilets is optional. Meeting the team's needs is imperative – that truly is what is meant as serving. Meeting the leader's needs is something totally different and not nearly as fulfilling – for anyone. What will your choice be?

Servant-leadership is not boastful, it is serving. Servant-leadership is not soft, it is powerful.

THE VIEW IS BREATHTAKING!

Truth freshly discovered or rediscovered is refreshing and exciting. However, discovering truth is not always easy. In Winston Churchill's words "Men stumble over the truth from time to time, but most pick themselves up and hurry off as if nothing happened." Churchill, as you probably know, was Prime Minister of England during WWII, and is credited with leading his country through an inspiring resistance effort that led to victory over Nazi Germany by the Allies.

How can the People Connection can be this good? Simple. It's in harmony with the way we're designed as human beings, and because of that it resonates with tremendous power. The principles used in the People Connection came from centuries of human experience, and from some of the greatest minds in history. This book is about what I have personally seen work. I have learned by trial and error, humbly accepting the gifts of criticism, and from observing the lowliest to the greatest among us and our ancestors. *It really is this good, because truth put to work is very powerful.*

Writers from all ages have given us many pieces of the truth we're looking for, but it's the Bible that gives us all of the truths the People Connection employs. The Bible says the truth will set us free. The truth contained in the People Connection will set us free from the oppressiveness of jobs so many of us have today. The Bible is unparalleled in its teachings on servant-leadership, vision, controlling our thoughts, and to how we are all members of one body, none more important than the other.

We can also look to nature. Many see God and the power of His creation by immersing themselves in the wilderness or the night sky. Profound and surprising lessons can be learned in doing this. One of these lessons follows:

The July 2007 National Geographic magazine contained an article entitled "Swarm Theory", which was also quoted in chapter 1. Scientists are hard at work trying to understand how creatures such as ants, bees, fish, birds, and animals can accomplish such amazing things by working together.

One scientist, Deborah Gordon, stated, "Ants aren't smart. Ant colonies are. A colony can solve problems unthinkable for individual ants, such as finding the shortest path to the best food source, allocating workers to different tasks, or defending territory from neighbors. As individuals, ants might be tiny dummies, but as colonies they respond quickly to their environment. They do it with something called swarm intelligence."[27]

The researchers are keenly interested in answering the question of how the simple actions of individuals can add up to the complex behavior of the group. For example, Thomas Seeley, a biologist at Cornell University, has been looking at the amazing ability of honeybees to make good decisions in spite of the many different opinions the 50,000 or so bees in a hive may have.

Bee hives normally split in late spring when the colony gets too crowded. The queen, some drones, and about half the workers leave the hive and camp out on a nearby tree branch. They send scouts to find a new home, which they expect to be exactly the right one since they will not move again. The research team set up an experiment involving five nest boxes, four that weren't quite big enough, and one that was about perfect.

"Scout bees soon appeared at all five," says Peter Miller, author of the article. "When they returned to the swarm, each performed a waggle dance urging the other scouts to go have a look. (These dances include a code giving directions to a box's location.) The strength of each dance reflected the scout's enthusiasm for the site. After a while, dozens of scouts were dancing their little feet off, some for one site, some for another, and a small cloud of bees was buzzing around each box.

"The decisive moment didn't take place in the main cluster of bees, but out at the boxes, where the scouts were building up. As soon as the number of scouts visible near the entrance to a box reached about 15 – a threshold confirmed by other experiments – the bees in that box sensed that a quorum had been reached, and they returned to the hive with the news. Scouts from the chosen box then spread through the swarm, signaling that it was time to move. Once all the bees had warmed up, they lifted off for their new home, which, to no one's surprise, turned out to be the best of the five boxes.

"The bees' rules for decision-making are to seek a diversity of options, encourage a free competition among ideas, and use an effective mechanism to narrow choices."[28]

Notice that like the ants and the caribou (in chapter 1), there is no one in charge. The queen lays the eggs, she doesn't call the shots.

"No generals command ant warriors. No managers boss ant workers. Even with a half million ants, a colony functions just fine with no management at all – at least none that we would recognize. Whether we're talking about ants, bees, pigeons, or caribou, *the ingredients of smart group behavior—decentralized control, response to local cues, simple rules of thumb—add up to a shrewd strategy to cope with* <u>*complexity*</u>*."*[29]

The ants, bees, and caribou operate in so many ways like the People Connection. The absence of a commander, the simple rules that work well in dealing with complexity, the responsible actions of individuals and the process for making group decisions compare exquisitely. And one last comparison, though symbolic, is that honey is the only food that never spoils. It has been found still good after thousands of years of being buried in the tombs of the Egyptian Pharaohs. The Bible uses the word "work" almost 700 times and delivers the message that God sanctified it. Our work, therefore, must have eternal significance, like honey.

I have often heard that anyone can make a subject complex, but it takes a genius to reduce it to elegant simplicity. Perhaps the ants, the bees, the caribou, and special human leaders and teams have benefited from a genius that we have deprived ourselves of for centuries.

The infinite power that created this incredible universe has lessons for all of us that can take us to heights we never dreamed possible.

INDEX

END NOTES

1 Miller, Peter; (July, 2007) Swarm Theory, National Geographic Magazine; pages 141 & 146.

2 Spherion in the News, Volume III; http://www.spherion.com/press/ press_coverage/v3.jsp Good news for job hoppers: Frequent change maintains passion, http://blog.penelopetrunk.com/2006/12/24/good-news-for-job-hoppers-frequent-change-maintains-passion

Spherion Study Shows Less Than Half of U.S. Workers Are Satisfied With Their Jobs; Benefits and Compensation Inadequate to Retain Employees,; http://www.spherion.com/pressroom/index.php?s=43&item=448

Spherion in the News, Volume II; http://www.spherion.com/press/ press_coverage/v2.jsp

Two-Thirds of Employees Want to Change Jobs Says New Research, (10/24/2006); http://www.hr.com/servlets/sfs?&t=/Default/gateway&i=111 6423256281&b=1116423256281&application=story&active=no&Parent ID=1119278002800&StoryID=1162134521544&xref=http%3A//www. google.com/search%3Fq%3DPeople+want+to+change+jobsw%26hl%3Den %26start%3D10%26sa%3DN

3 Scott Adams; Dilbert; 3/2/04 and 5/3/07.

4 Collins, Jim; (2001) Good to Great. New York, NY: HarperCollins; pages 1 – 3.

5 Ibid; pages 12, 13, and 14.

6 Imai, Masaaki; (1997) Gemba Kaizen. New York, NY: McGraw-Hill; page 16.

7 Deming, W. Edwards; (1992) Out of the Crisis. Cambridge, MA: Center for Advanced Engineering Study; pages 23 & 24.

8 Covey, Stephen R.: (1990) The 7 Habits of Highly Effective People. New York, NY: Fireside, page 241.

9 Deming, W. Edwards; (1992) <u>Out of the Crisis</u>. Cambridge, MA: Center for Advanced Engineering Study; pages 23 & 24.

10 Covey, Stephen R.: (1990) <u>The 7 Habits of Highly Effective People.</u> New York, NY: Fireside, page 235.

11 Deming, W. Edwards; (1992) <u>Out of the Crisis.</u> Cambridge, MA: Center for Advanced Engineering Study; pages 23 & 24.

12 Blanchard, Ken & Bowles, Sheldon; (1998) <u>Gung Ho!</u> New York, NY: William Morrow and Co., Inc. Page 99.

13 Collins, Jim; (2001) <u>Good to Great</u>. New York, NY: HarperCollins; pages 5 & 6.

14 Ibid; pages 164 & 165.

15 Ibid; page 169.

16 Deming, W. Edwards; (1992) <u>Out of the Crisis.</u> Cambridge, MA: Center for Advanced Engineering Study; pages 23 & 24.

17 Collins, Jim; (2001) <u>Good to Great.</u> New York, NY: HarperCollins; page 173.

18 Ibid; page 176 & 177.

19 Imai, Masaaki; (1997) <u>Gemba Kaizen.</u> New York, NY: McGraw-Hill; page 16.

20 Collins, Jim; (2001) <u>Good to Great.</u> New York, NY: HarperCollins; 173.

21 Ibid; page 12.

22 Ibid; pages 36 & 37.

23 Ibid; Pages 20 & 36.

24 Ibid; pages 36 & 37.

25 Ibid; page 22.

26 Blanchard, Ken & Hodges, Phil; (2003) <u>The Servant Leader</u>. Nashville, TN: J. Countryman; Page 68.

27 Miller, Peter; (July, 2007) Swarm <u>Theory, National Geographic Magazine</u>; page 130.

28 Ibid; page 138.

29 Ibid; page 130.

2096335

Made in the USA